BIGWIGS

Bigwig: A person of great importance, consequence, or dignity; a great or notable personage.

BIGWIGS

Canadians Wise and Otherwise

By Charles Vining
(R. T. L.)

WITH 37 ILLUSTRATIONS BY
IVAN GLASSCO

Essay Index Reprint Series

BOOKS FOR LIBRARIES PRESS, INC.
FREEPORT, NEW YORK

First Published 1935
Reprinted 1968

LIBRARY OF CONGRESS CATALOG CARD NUMBER:
68-16984

PRINTED IN THE UNITED STATES OF AMERICA

To One Called Susie

CONTENTS

EXPLANATION

"R. T. L." started in Toronto one afternoon seven years ago when I happened to sit down beside a friend at a table in Child's, an institution frequented for inspirational purposes by inmates of the old Toronto *Star* office, of whom I was one.

My friend's name was Joseph Easton McDougall and he was then editor of a humourous affair called *Goblin*. As the coffee gradually took effect Mr. McDougall became seized of the idea that I should supply his magazine with suitably informative descriptions of several Leading Citizens. The only obstacle seemed to be the impropriety of a Toronto *Star* man's name appearing in another publication, and young Mr. McDougall brushed this quickly aside by devising the signature R. T. L., initials which have no meaning as far as I know, although I have heard various interpretations of uncomplimentary character.

At any rate, R. T. L. duly executed for *Goblin* a series of sketches some of which, looking back at them with the sobriety of advancing years, were scandalously impertinent. A modified series later appeared in the Toronto *Star Weekly*, and with that R. T. L. would probably have lapsed into merited silence had he not been stirred to new and more ambitious activity in 1933 by Mr. H. Napier Moore, editor of *Maclean's* Magazine. The subjects in this book are those which have been published by *Maclean's* during the last two years, with a number of additions and revisions. Each sketch shows the date when it was written or revised, and I have not attempted changes to fit subsequent events because these occur too rapidly: yesterday's Capitalist may be Out for Reform to-morrow.

To Mr. Moore I tender my thanks for the fortitude with which he has met the occasional indignation of Constant Readers outraged by these irreverent references to persons of eminence and renown. There is no doubt that R. T. L. has been lacking in respect, and, although he has never been guilty of intended unkindness, I have had a great deal of trouble with him and am one of those in favour of his permanent suppression.

CHARLES A. M. VINING.

Montreal, January, 1935.

MR. ALLAN

December, 1934.

MR. GEORGE WILLIAM ALLAN, K.C., lives in Winnipeg and is one reason why people admit that men are men out there.

He regards it as an exaggeration to describe him as the Grand Old Man of the West because he did not settle in Winnipeg until several years after the Red River Rebellion and will not be seventy-five until next August.

He is Chairman of the Canadian Committee of the Hudson's Bay Company, a prehistoric institution which used to have a little difficulty in determining whether it was an arctic expedition, an outpost of Empire, a club for gentlemen or actually a commercial enterprise.

He is also president of Great West Life and a director of Canadian Bank of Commerce, Canada Cement, National Trust, British-American Oil and numerous other concerns which take him east often enough to make him glad he doesn't live there.

He is big, burly, bald and blunt, and vigorously objects to photographers on the ground that they always make him look like a great white bull.

He has a deep rumbling voice which matches his somewhat intimidating exterior but is never able to conceal his courtesy and kindness.

Allandale, Ontario, was named after his grandfather and the Allan Gardens in Toronto after his father, a senator and distinguished lawyer of that city. He himself was born in Moss Park, Toronto, but has always felt that this was not his fault.

He went to Upper Canada College for a while, relieved the situation by transferring to Galt Collegiate and conferred a favour there by transferring again to Trinity College School at Port Hope.

He managed to finish Trinity College School and, under this momentum, proceeded to Trinity College University,

3

studied law with the old Blake firm in Toronto and became a bachelor of arts in 1880, when he was twenty years old.

He thereupon departed for the West to employ these scholastic attainments by getting into the lumber business in Brandon when it was still in the tent-town stage.

He landed in Winnipeg two years later, found that lawyers were scarcer than lumber merchants and forthwith formed a legal firm which has now been in existence for fifty-two years.

He prospered quickly, thanks partly to the fact that, having attended so many different schools in Ontario, he had a wide circle of fellow alumni who knew no other lawyer in the West.

His early years as a legal luminary were spent chiefly travelling the prairies with tent and buckboard examining real estate possibilities for acquisitive gentlemen in the east, and he thus participated in the beginning of nearly every western city.

His activities at this time supply whatever factual basis there may be for the countless gargantuan legends which have made him the best smoking-room companion in the highly competitive western field.

He is probably the only man in Canada who can tell stories better than his fellow-citizen, Mr. E. H. Macklin, and nearly as well as the late Colonel George Ham.

To this talent he adds a judgment in the selection of good food which makes him a dinner host beyond any visible competition.

To him belongs chief credit for the delicate transitional operations by which the Hudson's Bay Company has gradually become a truly Canadian institution with the Canadian Committee something more than a decorative appendage.

His busiest time of the year occurs when the Governor of Hudson's Bay arrives from London for the annual visit, a period of social and other complexities horrible to contemplate.

Pressure of business duties prevented him from accompanying the Governor upon the voyage to the Company's Eskimo subjects last summer and it is now perhaps doubtful whether he will ever attain a title.

He is a prolific writer of letters to innumerable friends most of whom, by tacit agreement, do not trouble him by replying.

He is Conservative in politics but liberal in philosophy, a combination which has enabled him to emerge undamaged even from his sojourns at the Union Club in Victoria.

He usually spends the early spring weeks of each year at the Union Club and employs himself there with golf, bridge, cigars and correspondence dealing impolitely with the weather and other current topics.

He also belongs to the York Club in Toronto and the Rideau in Ottawa, but does not seem to mind.

He ventured actively into politics in 1917 and spent the next four years at Ottawa as the member for South Winnipeg. As a statesman he was highly useful to the Union Government, the usual procedure being that when something really difficult had to be managed he gave a dinner party.

He attends to his wardrobe by ordering a batch of clothes out from a London tailor every ten or fifteen years and has the faculty of always looking well dressed, although he never bothers to have anything pressed.

During the winter months in Winnipeg he wears a coonskin coat which is even frowsier than the specimen treasured in Montreal by Professor Stephen Leacock and, regardless of temperature, walks daily to his office.

For his office in Winnipeg he uses the Hudson's Bay board room where he sits, on the site of old Fort Garry, surrounded by portraits of historic gentlemen and unequipped with any desecrating telephone.

He likes things to be well-worn and comfortable, especially his friends.

MR. BEATTY

July, 1934.

MR. E. W. BEATTY is president of Canadian Pacific Railway Company, wears his hat on one side of his head and works most of the time.

He has a position which American newspapers have often described as the biggest business job in the world. He also takes part in running McGill, the Bank of Montreal, a hospital, a boys' training school, a trust company, several insurance corporations, various other enterprises and any charitable campaign that comes along.

He is called upon for assistance in matters ranging from an Imperial Economic Conference to a perplexed husband and treats these with equal effectiveness.

He is familiarly known, but seldom addressed, as Eddie. The members of his family have always called him Ned.

In physical appearance he is aggressive, but in behaviour he is tolerant and conciliatory even when he has to deal with newsprint executives.

The fault he forgives least readily is bumptiousness.

He was born in Thorold, Ontario, moved to Toronto when he was nine, and went in for law because his older brother chose medicine first.

It is popularly believed that he was ejected from every preparatory school he attended, but the less interesting truth is that he frequently stood first in his class.

He redeemed this error at Varsity, however, by finishing his Political Science course sixteenth in a class of eighteen, chiefly because he was taking an intensive course in football at the same time.

In football he was captain and quarter-back of Varsity Thirds, played in a Dominion final for the Seconds and might have made the First team had it not been for one, Mr. John Wilberforce Hobbs, a rotund, amiable and sagacious gentlemen who has been his closest friend ever since.

7

He finished law at Osgoode in 1901, eleventh in a class of forty, and went to Montreal that summer as an assistant in the Canadian Pacific's legal department at fifty dollars a month.

He became president of the C. P. R. in 1918, a few days before he was forty-one.

Twice during the seventeen years which intervened he nearly left the railway, once in 1908 to join a Toronto legal firm and again in 1912 to enter partnership with the persuasive Mr. W. N. Tilley.

He describes himself as a Continuing Presbyterian but this is a matter of inclination rather than performance.

He has no use for people who gossip or try to flatter him and finds that most women are apt to do both.

His nearest public approach to matrimony was his rumoured engagement some years ago to a young lady he had never seen.

He lived in boarding houses for his first sixteen years in Montreal and now owns a large house on Pine Avenue, to which he has added a squash racquets court as a means of exercise.

He has another house at Pointe Claire, where he lives from May to September and employs his friends at tennis with dour determination.

To keep physically fit he has retained, for over twenty years, the almost daily services of a cheerful individual named Mr. Pug Rennie, with whom he has engaged in various activities from boxing to running around Mount Royal.

His programme in recent years has been to confer with Mr. Rennie in the Pine Avenue house for an hour every evening before dinner, either at squash racquets or on the rubbing table.

After dinner, he usually goes upstairs to his library and does another day's work, during which he likes to have every light in the room turned on and the radio blaring.

He seldom goes to bed before midnight or one o'clock,

gets up with considerable reluctance about nine, and reaches his office about ten.

A leather brief-case full of work goes up from his office to the house every evening for his occupation. This is called for early each morning and the contents sorted out before he starts another day.

Since he finished school thirty-two years ago, there has been scarcely one evening during which he has not spent some time at work.

He will take a cocktail but no whiskey, and prefers a mild mixture of gin with soda and a slice of lemon.

During his early years in Montreal he frequently had dealings with a young Calgary lawyer who was engaged in C.P.R. work and whom he used to address as Mr. R. Buck-shot Bennett.

Among his frequent companions at luncheon are Sir Herbert Holt and Sir Charles Gordon, two citizens of Montreal noted for their lifelong indifference to monetary considerations.

He has many suits of clothes, but they are difficult to tell apart.

His chief amusements are double solitaire, billiards, poker, tennis and conversation. He does not play golf, although his vocabulary is admirably suited to the game's most trying moments.

He weighed one hundred and forty when he played football, tries now to keep down to one hundred and sixty-five or so, and finds this increasingly difficult.

He rarely laughs audibly but his grin is accepted as fully adequate.

Among his public errors was his 1931 prediction of an almost immediate end of the depression, an optimism highly distressing to one or two of the grimmer characters among his associates.

He will soon be fifty-seven and is almost never ill, although he has several times talked with Judge Fullerton.

IVAN
CLASICO

MR. BENNETT

January, 1933.

MR. RICHARD BEDFORD BENNETT, K.C., is a lawyer from Calgary who lately has neglected his practice.

He feels, however, that his present occupation is quite satisfactory as he meets so many interesting people and can always call a cabinet meeting when there is nothing important to be done.

Among the people he has met already are Mr. Stanley Baldwin and Mr. J. H. Thomas, two charming fellows who came all the way out from England last summer just to talk with him about the Empire.

He was able to agree with them perfectly as long as they gave him all he wanted, in which respect they were so obliging that the Conference was only once or twice on the verge of collapse.

He likes being Prime Minister and, if there now are times when he is not quite as pleased about it as he was two years ago, it is possible that he still feels more pleased than he will two years hence.

He considers that The Depression has got beyond a joke but perceives that some members of his cabinet have not.

He regards his ancestors with approval since they were so sagacious as to arrange that he be born under the British flag, a fact which has been of oratorical value almost ever since.

He was sixty-three years old last third of July (1932) and is prepared to prove that his birthday is not really the Fourth.

It is probable that no other Prime Minister since Confederation has been beset by so many problems and it is certain that no other has carried so many alone.

It is equally certain, even to those who oppose him most, that no Canadian of this generation has given himself more unsparingly to what he conceives to be the public interest.

11

He is usually in a hurry and feels uneasy when he is not.

He was born at Hopewell, New Brunswick, studied law at Dalhousie University, settled down in Chatham, New Brunswick, and became a member of the town council when he was twenty-seven.

He also taught in the Methodist Sunday School in Chatham and there met Joseph and Jennie Shirreff, from which humble beginning he found himself thirty years later possessed of half the Eddy Match Company.

He no longer teaches Sunday School but still admires the Scriptures and frequently refers to them without fear of contradiction.

He moved out to Calgary when he was twenty-eight, got himself elected to the Legislative Assembly a year or so later, became a Federal member in 1911 and has never since really escaped.

He belongs to the Ranchmen's Club in Calgary but is rather alarmed about horses and does not even ride a bicycle.

With anyone who is not too easily overawed he is a delightful companion and is at his best at a dinner party where there is a great deal of rapid conversation

He has an appropriately distinguished appearance, an impressive bulk, a faultless wardrobe and a commanding eye which has become more so since the summer of 1930.

He shuns tobacco and alcoholic beverages and hardly ever uses bad language because he prefers words with more syllables.

In his younger days he had a theory that it helped a politician to be known as a bit of a gay dog but has long since abandoned the idea as he had only indifferent success in trying to apply it.

He has prodigious mental capacity and an astoundingly accurate accumulation of heterogeneous information from which he is able to draw an instantaneous torrent of oratory upon any topic an opponent may care to mention.

He does not believe that discretion is the better part of valour and prefers the adage that he who hesitates is lost.

He is seldom afflicted by doubts as to the correctness of his conclusions and misguided obstruction to his plans is likely to induce an emotional metamorphosis which renders him as domineering and highly unpleasant as he has been affable and charming two minutes before.

He likes barber shops and wishes he could spend more time in them.

He was once inclined to attribute his success in life to himself and Senator Lougheed but later became less certain about the senator's contribution.

He has a talent for discovering things about people, an inclination to believe the unfavourable, and a genius for ultimate retribution.

He is an honorary colonel and a doctor of laws but it probably may be assumed that these titles are hardly worth using.

It pleases him to realize that he could almost anytime now become a peer of the realm and that in the House of Lords there are few noblemen, by birth or like Lord Beaverbrook, who could match him in eloquence and erudition.

He has small neat feet, walks with short rapid steps, and has never been quite as good a dancer as he once hoped to be.

When the war broke out he was one of those who helped organize Princess Patricia's Canadian Light Infantry, a distinction he values so highly that he has never emphasized it.

He has the quality of courage which burns brightest with necessity and is probably the most combative leader among our modern statesmen.

He is sentimental rather than romantic and has a disposition which finds satisfaction in martyrdom.

His instinct is to take a high moral stand on any question which provides the slightest excuse for doing so.

In this respect he is excelled only by Mr. Mackenzie King, a fellow-celibate who finds life a little dull these days.

13

SIR ROBERT

April, 1934.

SIR ROBERT BORDEN is an extremely distinguished old gentleman who lives in Ottawa and tries not to notice what is going on there.

Even in retirement he probably ranks as our most eminent living statesman, although a number of citizens feel that the competition is not very keen.

He entered politics when he was forty-two, was chosen as Conservative leader when he was forty-six and became Prime Minister at fifty-seven, which interfered with his golf.

He stayed as Prime Minister for nine years and when he retired in 1920 was the only head of a goverement still alive who had served continuously as such throughout the war.

He retired on account of broken health, will be eighty in June (1934) and is about due to be mentioned by the Toronto *Mail and Empire* as the next Conservative leader, should need arise.

He represented Canada at the Peace Conference in 1919, the Washington Conference in 1922 and the League of Nations in 1930. In between times he has acted as Chancellor of McGill and of Queen's, lectured at Toronto University and at Oxford and been president of various worthy societies.

To fill his spare time he has become head of Barclay's Bank and president of an insurance company, but has avoided trouble so assiduously that many people believe he died some years ago.

He was born in the Evangeline village of Grand Pré, Nova Scotia, and has been pleased to emphasize upon occasion that no member of his family has ever lived under any flag but the British.

He has traced his family back to a Kentish gentleman

of 1380 and has described his racial ingredients as two parts English, one part Scotch and one part Irish.

In spite of this imperialistic mixture he has been among the most ardent Canadians of his time and will be recorded in history as a chief architect of national independence.

In disposition he is modest and unassuming, this being a well-known characteristic of Conservative Prime Ministers.

He went to a private school called Acadia Villa Academy, replaced one of the masters at fifteen, spent a year teaching at Glenwood Institute in New Jersey and then settled in Kentville, Nova Scotia, to study law.

He was admitted to the Nova Scotia bar when he was twenty-four, practised in Kentville and then went to Halifax to join the famous Tory firm of Tupper, Thompson, Graham and Tupper.

Before he joined the firm he was a pronounced Liberal in support of his cousin, Sir Frederick Borden, but he absorbed considerable Conservatism with his law and found that both agreed with him.

He is probably the only Canadian who would be publicly acceptable as Governor-General, which may be a little disappointing to several intellectuals now waiting in the Senate.

He is also Honorary Colonel of the 63rd Regiment in Halifax, but does not expect to have to do much in the next war.

He was persuaded into politics by Sir Charles Tupper in 1896, with the understanding that he would stay for one season only.

After the next Conservative defeat in 1900 he was selected to replace Sir Charles as Conservative leader and reluctantly agreed to take the job for one year.

His selection for this honour was chiefly due to the fact that he was regarded as a good, safe man, which is a little like telling a girl that she has a nice, kind face.

He led the party to further defeats in 1904 and 1908, tried several times to resign but was compelled to stay because another victim could not be found.

He was, in consequence, highly indignant when he discovered a conspiracy to oust him on the verge of victory in 1911 and became sufficiently aroused to quelch this revolt with a vigour which astounded the gentlemen involved.

Observing this behaviour, the party strategists endeavoured to keep him aroused during the Reciprocity campaign of 1911 by planting hecklers in his audiences, with quite interesting results.

He won by forty-six seats in 1911 and then had a worse time with cabinet aspirants than he had ever experienced in defeat.

He moved to Ottawa to live in 1905 and gave up his law practice, probably realizing that to work for a living in Ottawa would be indelicate.

He was the first overseas minister of the Empire invited to attend a meeting of the British cabinet and went to London for that purpose in 1915.

He was accompanied by one of the new Western members of parliament, named R. B. Bennett, and was cajoled by this advisor into purchasing a wardrobe of London tailoring such as he had never owned before.

He is dignified, deliberate and discreet but once got into a religious revival meeting by mistake and fell asleep.

He likes to pretend that he pays no attention to the newspapers and has rarely been caught reading one in public.

He has seldom been disconcerted, although he was once engaged in conversation by an old lady who expressed open disappointment upon discovering that he was not the man who made condensed milk.

He still has thick, curly hair parted in the middle but his moustache is considerably more stream-lined than it used to be.

He has an invincible integrity which remains apparent even when he goes fishing.

MR. BRADSHAW

September, 1934.

MR. THOMAS BRADSHAW is Toronto's most imperviously
respectable citizen, which automatically gives him first place
in the whole country.

He can hardly expect admission of this by the Toronto
newspapers since he does not own a department store, has
never entertained the Governor-General and is not even a
United Empire Loyalist.

He ranks, however, as quite a creditable resident of the
city and is one reason why it is recognized as Toronto the
Good.

He is president of North American Life Assurance Company, a position having aspects of altruism suitable to his
philosophy. He has also been a financial authority and an
investment banker which have been demonstrated to be
two quite different things.

He is still an outstanding financial authority and in this
role has lately been to the rescue of various Canadian mun-
icipalities, a form of activity which affords him the same
satisfaction as a certain low type of mentality derives from
completing a grand slam doubled and vulnerable.

He does not smoke, drink, golf, gamble, go to movies,
and does not even want to.

He regards punctuality as one of the essential virtues and
will go to any lengths rather than be late for an engagement which usually means that he has to wait for people.

He believes that he has no use for acquiescent subordin-
ates, sometimes referred to as yes-men, and likes his young
men to battle with him as long as they do not make the unfortunate error of attempting to obstruct something he
really wants.

In spite of his gentle manner and almost saintly coun-
tenance he possesses considerable warmth of temper, control of which places him under a severe strain as he lacks
a working knowledge of the words commonly employed
for emotional relief.

Upon losing his temper he never fails to make generous amends and, having done so, is quite likely to return at once to the dispute with increasing emphasis.

He usually has lunch at the National Club, a Toronto institution on Bay Street noted for the high intellectual standard of its inmates.

He was born in England, came out to Canada to make his living when he was twelve years old, and is so modest that it embarrasses him to admit even to himself the success he has since achieved.

He settled in Toronto and got his first job as a cash boy in Eaton's store, an enterprise renowned for its benevolent practices.

He stayed with this for a few months and then, at thirteen, became a printer's devil at the Mail Printing Company which now produces a journal called the *Mail and Empire*, read by a number of Toronto citizens for the complete impartiality of its political utterances.

From this print shop he carried copy to the newly formed North American Life where he made such a favourable impression that he was persuaded to sign on as office boy for three years.

By this promotion he secured a salary of five dollars a month and was given a bonus for going to night school and learning shorthand, an educational adventure which so stimulated his ambition that he decided to acquire university training and become a doctor.

To carry out this resolution he had financial resources of five cents a day with which he was supposed to purchase his lunch. He went without lunch for six months, hired a tutor to coach him for matriculation, passed his examinations at first attempt and thus entered Varsity.

As a matter of monetary necessity he continued to work at North American Life in his spare time, an arrangement which ended in a very complete nervous collapse. He thereupon decided to abandon education and go in for finance.

He was slightly delayed in achieving this purpose, but,

after sixteen years with North American Life and another fourteen with Imperial Life, entered the investment banking business as a partner of Mr. A. E. Ames, an eminent Toronto citizen whom many people have unjustly mistaken for Sir Joseph Flavelle.

He got twenty-five thousand a year with Mr. Ames, but after five years of it, was so seized with public spirit that he accepted an appointment as Finance Commissioner of Toronto at fifteen thousand.

He stayed there for four years, succeeded in straightening out city finances in spite of the city council, and was then induced to join Massey-Harris Limited where he remained for ten years as general manager and ten months as president.

In 1926 he was instrumental in saving Massey-Harris from American control although this involved assistance from Mr. J. H. Gundy, a capitalist of the merger era who proceeded to re-finance the company for the public benefit.

He duly appreciated Mr. Gundy's efforts and found the experience quite educational.

He became president of North American Life in 1928, conducted the duties of this office by remote control for a couple of years, but left Massey-Harris at the end of 1930 to give full time to insurance.

He succeeded in mutualizing North American Life in 1931 and is now perfectly happy in spite of some of the company's distinguished directors.

In the last three years he has developed the company's business in most gratifying manner and has erected a highly impressive head office building, now popularly referred to as Uncle Tom's Cabin.

He has established in the new building an extensive library where he likes to find his bright young men engrossed and where new employees are obliged to take a course of study, whether they can read or not.

He no longer goes to the office at five-thirty in the morning as he finds it almost as convenient to work at home.

MR. BURTON

September, 1934.

MR. C. L. BURTON is president of Simpson's and doesn't care who knows it.

His first name is Charles and his second name is Luther but he rarely has time to use either.

As a Leading Citizen of Toronto he comes close to Doctor Cody, in spite of the fact that he is under the handicap of having to be at his office now and then.

He is there enough, at any rate, to permit no doubts among his young men as to where all the good ideas come from.

He occasionally takes a walk around the outside of the store to see if the windows have been well cleaned and always discovered that he could do them much better himself.

He is no more interested in what Eaton's are doing than he is in his right eye and he does not care any more about the store's daily sales total than he does about what Eaton's are doing.

He has an opinion on anything you might care to mention and, if you don't mention anything, you are the chief loser.

He once described the present government as picayune and has remarked for publication that Mr. Bennett's advisors have about as much wisdom as an alley cat.

This declaration had, of course, no reference to his favourite statesman, Mr. Harry Stevens, a seeker of the truth who is now one of our best-known authors.

He finds in Mr. Stevens the only subject on which he and Mr. R. Y. Eaton have ever agreed with any real enthusiasm.

He believes that everyone should learn to speak two languages before they bother about arithmetic.

He speaks two himself, and often.

He is fifty-eight years old and is pleased to realize that

23

he still has more pep than any of the young fellows around the store.

He often wonders what is wrong with young men these days anyway.

He did not start at Simpson's until he was thirty-six but has not lost much time since and is beginning to wonder what he had better fix up next.

He thinks traffic in Toronto and Hamilton is worse than in any American city and cannot understand why in the world the mayor and council don't fix it.

He once wrote a letter to the mayor about it but still nothing has been done.

He never goes anywhere without learning something and he is going somewhere all the time.

He wrote a letter to Mr. Mackenzie King before the last election and told him what he ought to do. He admits that Mr. King lost the election because this advice was not taken.

He feels obliged to have lunch in the store now and then to demonstrate how good it is.

By some peculiar method of his own he has convinced nearly everyone in the store, from gent's underwear to house furnishings, that he know everything that is going on at any minute of the day.

He reads everything the newspapers say about him and believes it as long as it is favourable.

He is direct and definite in his business dealings and avoids office ceremony, in which he differs from some of the young men he has employed.

He ventured into the publishing business about three years ago with results which lead to the conclusion that he may be pretty good at merchandising.

He is always ready to follow sound advice provided it conforms to his own ideas.

He likes to get several meetings going at one time in different offices and then drop in on each one just long enough to decide everything.

He believes that Canada could have twenty-five million

people in the next twenty-five years if the government and the railways had sense enough.

He thinks all war debts should be cancelled and, while this is not entirely an original idea, he still favours it.

He is president of the Big Brothers, which he enjoys, although he would enjoy it more if the name were changed to Bigger and Better.

He has become quite a horseman in recent years but has sometimes wished that it were not necessary.

He once suggested that the railways give a half-price return fare in the month of November so that Canadians could move around and see their country and does not accept the suggestion that anyone leaving Toronto might not use the second half of the ticket.

He has not yet tried writing poetry but is quite confident that he could if he wanted to, especially since he read Sir Thomas White's.

He does a great deal of good where it is most needed and this is one of the things he does not talk about.

He carries a small memo book with him and writes notes to himself. This is really unnecessary, as he never leaves anything undone long enough to forget it.

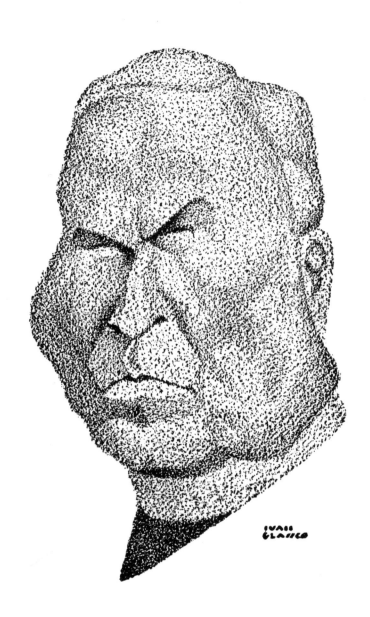

CANON CODY

March, 1933.

CANON CODY is president of Toronto University and now will probably never become Archbishop of Canterbury.

He does not, however, allow this limitation to make him unappreciative of his present lot.

He is Toronto's most persistent Leading Citizen and sits at more head-tables than any other notable of the city, with the possible exceptions of General Mitchell and Sir William Mulock, to whom that day is counted lost which does not bring at least one meal in public.

He has not reached the university standard of discretion, which requires one to be able to converse for two hours without making a statement, but he is safe enough in spite of the Toronto papers.

The first member of his family to visit Toronto arrived with the American troops in 1812 and liked the place so well that he came back later to settle there.

He likes Toronto, and as a natural product of that city ranks with Mr. George Young, Danforth Avenue on Saturday night, King Street on Sunday, the Beardmore boys, the Albany Club and the Old Union Station.

He owes his success in life to immunity from indigestion, an adjustable enthusiasm, an affable acquaintance with the right people and many sterling qualities.

He went through Galt Collegiate and University of Toronto, where he was a zealous member of the Literary and Scientific Society.

He was ordained as an Anglican priest in 1894 and immediately became curate of St. Paul's, which a number of Toronto people regard as the only church a governor-general can attend without demeaning himself.

He was curate of St. Paul's for five years, acting rector for eight years and rector for twenty-five, during which time he preached there whenever his engagements would permit.

Before he went to St. Paul's he helped to found an educational institution at St. Catharines, Ontario, known as Ridley College and stuck it out as classical master there for four years.

He also helped to found Havergal College for young ladies but has not yet taught there.

He was away from St. Paul's for about a year as Minister of Education for Ontario. This was not long enough for him to complete his educational plans but was quite sufficient to establish his political dexterity.

He has since then been an ex-officio member of every Ontario cabinet except that presided over by Mr. Ernest Drury, an exponent of democracy who lately appears to have abandoned the province to its fate.

It is not yet quite clear whether he was the best clergyman in politics or the best politician in the clergy but it is probably indisputable that he has been the most accomplished diplomat in either profession.

Among the other things he has been are colonel of the militia and vice-president of the Canadian Council of the Pocket Testament League.

He is also a member of Lambton Golf and Country Club, but is more active at Rotary, Kiwanis, Lions, Gyro, Board of Trade and any civic function of inauguration, dedication, presentation or supplication.

He is an adept at either welcome or farewell to Distinguished Visitors, private or public, athletic or cinematic, transatlantic or sub-American, literate or illiterate, and is so truly clever that he knows enough to subordinate his intelligence to the occasion.

Among the things he could have been if he had wanted to are Bishop of Nova Scotia and Archbishop of Melbourne, Australia. He turned these down because he felt that Toronto needed him, which appears to have been a mutually accurate diagnosis with highly satisfactory results.

He is always sufficiently informed of current events to be able to deliver appropriate remarks anywhere, at any time, on any subject, and understands the Toronto mind better than anyone else except Mr. Allan Ross who does not mean to but cannot help it.

He likes ripe olives.

Among the things he would have been good at, but has not yet been, are mayor of Toronto and Lieutenant-Governor of Ontario.

He is sixty-five now (1933) and is pleased that he has become president of the university before retirement age.

He has never paid any public tribute to his supposed relationship to the Colonel Cody who is better known as Buffalo Bill, and there has been nothing in his conduct to date which would serve to establish a family resemblance.

He has narrow grey eyes, acquisitive nose, mouth to match and small, neat handwriting.

He has never permitted his high intellectual attainments to blunt the sharp point of practical perceptions.

A large number of people have reason to be grateful to him because he believes that a friend is for help in trouble, and he is never too busy to translate this belief into action.

He once preached a sermon to Their Majesties in the private chapel at Buckingham Palace and has also acted as chaplain to the Bishop of London, which is something like being deputy to Mr. Bennett.

The London episodes were probably the greatest hours of his life and nothing now is likely to surpass them unless titles return to Canada.

SIR ARTHUR

(This sketch was written a few months before
Sir Arthur Currie's death, and is included
here because of my admiration and respect
for a great Canadian.—C. V.)

June, 1933.

SIR ARTHUR CURRIE is principal of McGill University
and a director of the Bank of Montreal, but makes the best
of things.

When life becomes too irksome he can always stir up
excitement by making a speech of political flavour.

He delivered a few remarks in 1924 about governmental extravagance, and was immediately suspected of preparing to displace Mr. Meighen as Conservative leader.

He made another speech this spring in favour of national government and is now suspected of conspiring to
do away with Mr. Bennett.

His fellow conspirators are believed to be certain prominent gentlemen whose modesty impels them to remain in
the background, which automatically eliminates Sir Henry
Drayton and ex-Senator McDougald.

He is six feet four inches high and used to weight 240
pounds, which entitled anyone under the rank of sergeant-
major to refer to him in terms of descriptive dis-respect.

He was born in Ontario in a place called Napperton,
went west when he was eighteen, taught school, sold insurance, and got into the real estate business in Victoria.

He also got into the militia, trained with the Garrison
Artillery for fifteen years, and transferred to the infantry
in 1913 to organize the Gordon Highlanders of Canada.

He was thirty-eight when war broke out, and went
across in September, 1914, in command of the Second
Brigade.

He had his first taste of wartime politics when he became
Major-General of the First Division in September, 1915,
and was ordered to make an appointment he did not favour.

He discovered a great deal more about politics when he

became Corps Commander in June, 1917, and was told what Ottawa expected of him in return. His refusal to comply was followed by a campaign of slander against him which spread throughout the army and persisted for ten years.

The slanderers did more harm to the country than to him because they kept him out of public life.

He took a canvas bathtub with him all over France, and was sitting in it when the Armistice order arrived. This seemed quite unpatriotic to some of the more warlike spirits at home.

His special order of March, 1918, to "Canadians, in this fateful hour" was regarded by British papers as finer than any of Napoleon's exhortations and has been used by the French in their schools. Apparently, however, it lost some of its appeal in coming across the Atlantic.

He made the Canadian Corps the greatest fighting machine on the Western front and was probably the outstanding British commander during the last hundred days of the war.

He was kept in London for a while to receive various honours before coming home in 1919 and made two speeches which caused London journals to describe him as the greatest Canadian of the generation.

The London *Times* was so unrestrained as to call him Canada's Man of the Hour and predict that this country could not afford to leave unused the high abilities of statesmanship which he had demonstrated.

Unfortunately there was some fear in Ottawa minds that the wrong political party might benefit by his services, and the strategists of that day met the danger by removing him from all activity with an appointment as Inspector-General of Militia.

This brought him under the ministerial authority of Mr. Hugh Guthrie, a political ambidexter now immured in Mr. Bennett's cabinet, and he soon suffered from acute nausea induced by overdoses of party patronage.

He resigned within a few months to become principal of McGill and has been there ever since, in spite of efforts to shanghai him aboard the ship of state under various captains.

Many people think he might still save the country from its politics if he were not so old, although actually he is younger that either Mr. Bennett or Mr. King and nearly as young as Mr. E. W. Beatty, none of whom has yet reached the age of matrimony.

He was a Liberal before the war, but nobody, including himself, has known his subsequent politics.

Apart from his unpleasant experience as Inspector-General, the only reward for his services to the country has been a long period of ill-health. This was not assisted by continued slander which a jury at Cobourg finally silenced in 1928.

For a considerable period after he went to McGill he subsisted chiefly on milk and orange juice, but later returned to pre-war beverages.

He lives in a huge house on McTavish Street, owned by the university, and feel apologetic about the ballroom.

His use of profanity is ingenious and effective but not as damaging as the quiet words he uses in stripping the epidermis from one who has been careless.

He can eat with chopsticks and is proud of the accomplishment.

He has never hesitated to disobey an order which he knew was wrong, whether it came from a field marshal, a bank president or a politician.

He is deeply emotional and has trouble with his tears when he is stirred.

His philosophy is that if you do what is right everything will come out straight in the end but he is a little sorry that sometimes it takes so long.

He is one of the few really great men this country has.

MR. DAFOE

October, 1933.

MR. JOHN W. DAFOE is editor of the Winnipeg *Free Press*, a high-minded journal which never swerves from the path of strict independence except to defend Liberal principles.

He has been described as the last of the great Canadian editors but nobody on the *Free Press* knows who the others have been.

He has a notable friend and colleague in the person of Mr. E. H. Macklin, a gentleman of great capacity whose health and vocabulary have been constantly improving for over seventy years.

Among his other colleagues are the Sifton brothers who own the paper and whom he appreciates as being very good with horses.

His ancestors were Flemish people who settled in New York in 1740. They called themselves Deffaux but had changed to Dafoe by the time they became United Empire Loyalists.

He has acquired a pleasantly protuberant middle.

He was brought up on a backwoods farm near Ottawa, went to high school in Arnprior and then started to teach school himself, equipped with a set of opinions as hardshell Orange and Tory as any young man's could be.

He taught a country school in the Ottawa Valley and took over his deceased predecessor's library which happened to consist chiefly of pamphlets containing the Free Trade teachings of Cobden and Bright.

By the time he had digested these he was a Free Trader himself and had so enjoyed the metamorphosis that he gave up teaching, packed his carpet bag and travelled to Montreal to ask for a job at the Montreal *Star*, which shows how innocent a young man can be at seventeen.

The pamphlets are still in the library in Winnipeg and he looks at them now and then when he begins to weaken.

He was such a perfect picture of rural ineptitude that the *Star* sent him to call on some crooked clothing merchants, who swindled him thoroughly and thus supplied him with the story which started him as a reporter.

He spent the next nineteen years in Montreal except for an interval as editor of the Ottawa *Journal*, which could not be regarded as much improvement and a temporary experiment with the Winnipeg *Free Press* during which he managed to obtain a scoop on the death of Sir John A. Macdonald by being friendly with the government telegraph operator.

He is a Doctor of Laws but nobody calls him Doctor except visiting Englishmen, who imagine that he likes it.

He took a hand in Sir Wilfrid Laurier's arrival as prime minister in 1896 by arranging publication of Father Lacombe's famous letter on the Manitoba School question, with satisfactorily explosive effect upon Ontario voters.

He reads everything he comes across, including newspapers, novels, magazines and biography, and has even been observed looking at the Toronto papers.

He was thirty-six when Sir Clifford Sifton invited him to return to the *Free Press* as editor. He went there in 1902 and has felt better ever since.

He made the *Free Press* a straight Liberal party organ for a number of years and threatened to resign rather than join Sir Clifford in breaking with Laurier over reciprocity in 1911.

By 1917, however, his party enthusiasm had waned sufficiently to disagree with Laurier on conscription and he was a prime mover in bringing about Union government.

For this activity he was offered a title but declined it on the ground that he looked after his own furnace, an impediment which several eminent citizens today would not regard as at all serious.

He knows hundreds of people and writes letters to most of them.

His hair, which used to be quite red, has become sandy

but is still even thicker and shaggier than the O'Cedar mop worn by Professor Stephen Leacock.

He also resembles Mr. Leacock in sartorial detail, his general appearance being still a little reminiscent of his arrival at the Montreal *Star* office fifty years ago.

When the Union government disappointed him by dissolving into Conservatism in 1920, he refused to return to the Liberal party and assisted the rise of the Progressives.

This experiment satisfied him only temporarily and by 1925 he felt obliged to support Liberalism again as the least of his available evils, although he has been so generous as to rank Mr. Arthur Meighen among the five greatest Canadians.

His support of Liberalism was assured in 1927 when the Conservative convention chose Mr. Bennett as leader, Mr. Bennett happening to be not one of his favourite statesmen.

He has, in fact, no favourite statesman and it is unlikely that he would be greatly distressed if Mr. Mackenzie King were replaced by Mr. Ralston or Mr. Massey, but not by Mr. Dunning, an attitude and distinction which all of the gentlemen concerned have probably not yet fully perceived.

He refuses to believe that a newspaper's editorial page has any less influence than it used to have.

His method of conducting an editorial campaign is to give small doses, but to give them often.

He believes it impossible to combine labour and farmers in a Third Party and consequently attaches little importance to the C.C.F., which he estimates will eventually recruit more from urban Conservatives than from Liberals.

He regards Mr. Woodsworth as a very nice man.

He has expressed his present greatest hope as being that Mr. Bennett will continue to lead the Conservative party until the next election campaign is over.

He longs for the fun to start.

SIR HENRY

May, 1934.

SIR HENRY LUMLEY DRAYTON is a resident of Toronto who has sometimes worked quite hard and is now retired, but not retiring.

He has very nice clothes, wears a jaunty hat, carries a stick, keeps a flower in his lapel and, under pressure, will admit that he is a handsome man.

At various times he has been rumoured as leader of the Conservative party, Lieutenant-Governor of Ontario, High Commissioner in London and head of Canadian National Railways, but none of these has yet quite happened.

He has several times, however, been a cabinet minister and, for a few days in 1926, substituted for Mr. Meighen as leader of the government in the House of Commons, a role in which his appearance was almost perfect.

He also had a pleasant interval as head of the Liquor Control Board in Ontario for which he received twenty thousand a year and a fund of anecdotes for dinner parties.

He believes that it is the duty of a government to practise strict economy, especially when he is out of office.

He did admirable work for the country during the war and in 1917 returned a government cheque for fifteen thousand dollars rather than take payment for patriotic services. Somehow or other this got into the papers.

His hair is nice and thick and he parts it nearly in the middle.

The high peak in his life thus far has been his appointment as Chief Commissioner of the Railway Board at forty-three. The low point was probably in Winnipeg when he received one vote as prospective Conservative leader at fifty-seven.

He was born in Kingston, Ontario and once was elected to parliament from there.

He used to have a drooping, luxuriant moustache which

was later trimmed to a bristly, military model and finally, in 1924, was shaved off entirely.

When he shaved off his moustache he had to have a lot of new photographs taken but did not mind.

He considers that he looks better clean-shaven but occasionally toys with the idea of growing a beard.

He has a great many friends, most of whom think well of him and was once able to attend a Liberal picnic in Quebec with no unfortunate result beyond circulation of a hope that he would soon become Conservative leader.

He was knighted on the King's birthday in 1915 and sometimes likes to sigh for the humble days when they just called him Harry.

He was once corporation counsel for Toronto, succeeded Mr. Hartley Dewart as crown attorney for the county of York, and became a King's Counsel but has never been obliged to let legal practice inconvenience him.

He is friendly and generous and does his best to be modest.

Beneath his bonhomie he has always been highly ambitious and firmly believes in the extreme importance of whatever he is doing.

Whenever he takes a new job he wants to change things and is a reformer by nature, in the sense that he realizes he can do things better than his predecessor.

He has belonged to more clubs than any other man in Canada except Herbert Molson and is a cheerful sportsman. He tries to be cheerful no matter what happens.

Quite a number of people have assured him that he would do awfully well in the movies and he has wondered sometimes if he shouldn't try.

In talking to a new acquaintance he is apt to mention casually that his old football knee is bothering him again.

One of his most notable efforts was the Drayton-Acworth report on the railway problem, which would probably have been an excellent thing for the country if it had been followed.

The report is still highly regarded by many people, including himself.

He has never ranked as a particularly good speaker, although he has a lovely platform manner and a number of splendid gestures.

He is at his best sitting in a club lounge with a prosperous cigar, explaining his opinions to men not quite as important as himself.

He is a chronic sentimentalist but likes to believe that he is a man of the world and very hard-boiled.

His manner at times is inclined to be coy but he has never been accused of timidity in the face of difficulty.

He is rather glad to be out of politics just now because he thus enjoys a greater freedom in discoursing upon errors of administration and he almost hopes that Mr. Bennett will not have to call upon him to save the country.

If called upon, however, he will do his best, for the sincerity of his Canadianism is one item of his inventory which few people would question.

He used to keep his name out of the telephone directory but has not found this necessary in recent years.

He believes that he leads a very strenuous life and is worried if he does not get eight hours' sleep every night.

He went to school in England and sometimes has found this difficult to forget.

He has occasionally pondered upon the ingratitude of mankind but feels, on the whole, that he has not been entirely overlooked in the distribution of tangible appreciation even though he has not yet had a trip to Geneva.

He is now nearly sixty-five years old and consoles himself with the reflection that in another few years he may be regarded as eligible for the senate.

He likes to talk about his health.

He is glad to be a hail-fellow-well-met because it depresses him to feel that anyone dislikes him. It also perplexes him.

He has a charming smile which he uses for that purpose.

MR. DUNNING

October, 1934.

MR. CHARLES AVERY DUNNING is willing to become a bank president if he has to but would first like to make sure that he is not going to be Prime Minister.

For the last four years or so he has been engaged in trying to accumulate a little money so that he may be suitably prepared for the second of these alternatives should he be forced to accept it.

His monetary endeavours have included the Seigniory Club and the Ontario Equitable. He has also practised a bit as a business doctor but has found that most of his patients really needed an undertaker.

He has recently become president of Maple Leaf Milling, from which some observers deduce that he has finished with politics while others conclude that he has merely found a better jumping-off place.

He was born in Croft, Leicestershire, started to work when he was eleven, and came out to Canada at seventeen after straining his heart in a swimming race.

His first job in Canada was with a farmer near Yorkton, Saskatchewan, at ten dollars a month and the farmer soon fired him for being no good.

He walked from Yorkton to Beaverdale, took up a homestead of 160 acres, bought a yoke of oxen, built himself a sod hut, and started to farm on his own. His living expenses for the first winter totalled seventeen dollars.

Most people call him Charlie, whether they approve of him or not.

When the Saskatchewan Grain Growers' Association had its first convention in Regina the Beaverdale farmers sent him as their delegate. He earned his board at the Regina hotel by stoking the furnace and slept in the boiler room.

At the psychological moment he gave the convention a fighting speech and was thereupon elected a director of the Association.

43

He did so well at this that he was picked a couple of years later to organize the Saskatchewan Co-operative Elevator Company. He was twenty-six then and, before he was thirty, had made this Company the largest single marketer of grain in the world.

In avoiding unpleasant people and in dodging unwanted engagements he is even more skilful than Mr. Mackenzie King, which is saying a great deal.

He has never learned how to make his tie look quite right, regards clothes as troublesome necessities, and is unofficially reported to have played golf at the Seigniory Club in his suspenders.

Nobody has ever been able to question his four-letter fortitude.

In 1916 he decided to become a statesman so he left the Saskatchewan Co-operative and joined the provincial government as treasurer.

Sir Wilfrid Laurier advised him to keep out of politics until he had made some money but he thought this unimportant , became premier of Saskatchewan when he was thirty-seven, went to Ottawa as Minister of Railways when he was forty-one, and was Minister of Finance at forty-four.

He was the youngest Minister of Finance in Canadian history and found himself in some danger of never quite getting over it.

He derives a Napoleonic pleasure from maps, which he used to like to spread in front of him when expounding railway matters to newspaper writers.

When he was beaten in the 1930 election he perceived that Sir Wilfrid had been right as his financial status at the end of fourteen years in politics consisted chiefly of debts.

He has since rid himself of these and it is improbable that he will return to politics until he has acquired an adequate financial cushion, which he may manage to accomplish just at the proper time.

He repudiates the report that he likes kippered herring.

44

Among his political recollections are the workings of the Saskatchewan Liberal Machine as operated by Mr. James G. Gardiner, a party engineer of single-track technique.

His regard for Mr. Gardiner is equalled only by the mutual esteem enjoyed by Mr. Harry Stevens and Mr. R. Y. Eaton.

He smokes expensive English tobacco which he obtains in cartridge form and loads into his pipe by means of a silver pocket gadget.

He prepares speeches with great care and on occasion has primed himself the night before by reading passages of Macaulay in order to get a free flow of English.

He has cultivated the oratorical device of laughing when angered and used to employ this to the intense irritation of Mr. Arthur Meighen.

His four years in the cabinet at Ottawa could hardly be described as happy and it is unlikely that he would again take office without certain changes among his colleagues.

He has, however, refrained from joining the Liberal group who would like to hasten the alteration process and has declined to abet convention plans for that purpose.

If circumstances happen to leave the leadership vacant. it is not impossible that he would feel it his duty to yield to sufficient pressure properly applied.

He would not serve under Mr. Bennett, even if invited, but there have been times when he might have consentd to save the country in a National Government with Mr. Rhodes.

His chief political deficiency is his inability to measure unfavourable opinions of himself and he probably has not yet fully discovered the western suspicions of his Montreal affiliations.

He also lacks the ability to procrastinate, so essential to professional politicians, and cannot let go of a difficulty until he has found a solution.

MR. FERGUSON

March, 1934.

MR. G. HOWARD FERGUSON is Canadian High Commissioner in London, and is thus entirely removed from politics except when something attracts his attention.

Being High Commisssioner is not quite what he once hoped he might become but it has at least enabled him to demonstrate what he could do to help Downing Street through the depression.

He went over for that purpose in the fall of 1930, and although England went off the gold standard a year later it is understood that very few people have held him responsible.

He shrinks from any form of publicity as a sunflower shrinks from the sun.

In spite of a net displacement of 218 pounds, he has managed to skate over considerable areas of thin ice without a single mishap.

Apart from this activity, he takes no exercise whatever if he can avoid it.

When he makes a mistake he is always indignant that people will not realize he was only joking.

Two of his rules of life are to find some humour in every situation and never to worry about anything and thus far he has rarely been without opportunity to test both rules fully.

He makes a good speech when the spirit moves him.

He owes his achievement to a hearty manner, an impenetrable epidermis and his wife.

He was born in a place called Kemptville, Ontario, stayed there until he was seventeen and then went to Toronto, to take arts at Varsity and law at Osgoode Hall.

He wears his hat on one side of his head and smokes a cigar the same way.

He likes barbers who talk to him.

After Osgoode, he went back to Kemptville, stayed there for another eleven years, and might be there still if a man in the village had not twitted him about his political manners.

He felt so twitted that he ran in the Ontario election of 1905 to show what he could do, managed to win, and continued this performance for the next twenty-five years, during which the audience had scarcely a dull moment.

In 1912, for example, he put on an entertaining act when he served as Dominion Commissioner enquiring into Trent Valley Canal affairs. Acting as a commissioner while also a member of the Ontario Legislature made him liable to a penalty of $2,000 a day, but he ended, instead, by being promoted to the Cabinet.

Another amusing skit was the Timber Probe of 1920, when he engaged in a public jiujitsu exhibition with Mr. Ernest Drury and was rewarded by getting the leadership of his party, instead of something much less pleasant.

In 1923 he played charades, for some months, with both the Wets and the Drys, but nobody could guess what word he meant so they elected him premier of the province to find out.

Throughout his twenty-five years in Ontario's public life he served the people with absolutely no motives of self-interest as long as he did what he wanted.

He fully realized that he was a statesman, and was constantly annoyed by Mr. Arthur Meighen, who treated him as merely another provincial premier.

He squared matters with Mr. Meighen at the Winnipeg convention, climbed aboard Mr. Bennett's band-wagon with his own bass drum, gave the campaign the gusto it needed, and was confident that he would be suitably rewarded.

He was considerably perturbed when Mr. Bennett failed to take a similar view of the situation in 1930. He succeeded in getting the London appointment chiefly because Mr. Bennett's first choice for this honour delayed too long about accepting it.

He managed, however, to make the London appointment sound something like a coronation, and made a modest exit from Ontario by announcing that he had given enough time to the trifling affairs of the province and, henceforth, would devote himself to saving England from decadence.

He found it difficult to make Mr. Bennett perceive the humour of these remarks and left for England with a feeling that the Prime Minister was, perhaps, just a little displeased with him.

Mr. Bennett confirmed this suspicion by severely ignoring him for his first couple of years in England, which was quite long enough for Mrs. Ferguson to make her husband almost as popular in London as he had once been in Toronto.

He is now so far restored to Mr. Bennett's favour that the Right Honourable gentleman has even mentioned him as a possible successor, although without any visible delight on the part of certain Cabinet members.

He pretends to be impulsive.

He likes to come back to this country for a holiday and tell the newspapers what Premier Henry is going to do.

He was appropriately moved when Premier Henry presented Senator Meighen with a remunerative job on the Hydro Commission, and still hopes that if the senator ever gets into trouble it will be nothing trivial.

One of his best meals is breakfast.

He will be sixty-four in June (1934) just about the time the next batch of Canadian aristocrats will be announced, unless it occurs to the Government that this may not be the best strategy in the world with an election in the offing.

He is not quite certain whether he is now in line for a title himself but considers that he is probably as patrician as some of the country's present noblemen.

He does not wish, however, to be unduly forward about this and would be fully satisfied with something simple, such as the Duke of Kemptville or perhaps Count Abitibi.

At present most people call him Fergy.

MR. GARDINER

July, 1934.

MR. JAMES GARFIELD GARDINER is a young man who went west and now hopes sometime to move east again.

He quite enjoys being Premier of Saskatchewan but would not refuse a position really worthy of his talents and, in this respect, agrees that Ottawa might properly be regarded as a suitable setting.

He will be fifty-one this fall (1934) and has definitely made up his mind to retire from politics when he is older.

He has moved his political supporters to a devotion so intense that any personal comment of a non-eulogistic nature renders them disposed to immediate violence.

Those who are less devoted feel that his breadth of political outlook approximates the lateral dimension of the tenement house hall in New York where a dog is obliged to wag his tail up and down.

It is generally admitted, however, that he is completely non-partisan as long as no question of party advantage is involved.

He was born on a farm near Exeter, Ontario, learned an early lesson in agricultural arithmetic and left with his family when he was six to settle on new land in Nebraska.

The farm in Nebraska proved just as profitable as the one in Ontario and his family returned home in 1896 on the general principle that if they were going to starve they might as well have British burial.

He worked for a neighbour for the next four years, managed to save enough money to buy a one-way harvesters' ticket to the west and went out when he was seventeen to work for an uncle at Clearwater, Manitoba.

He loved being a harvester but, when the season was over, felt that he should do something about his cultural development which had come to a full stop in Grade Seven of Public School.

Ten years later, at the age of twenty-seven, he had

completed various stages of scholastic endeavour **and** graduated from Manitoba College as a fully equipped bachelor of arts.

He was also pretty well equipped as a political orator by persistent emulation of one of his school-teachers, a worthy gentleman named Harvey Greenway, who ranked as a spellbinder of considerable renown.

He followed Mr. Greenway still further by securing the job of school principal at Lemberg, Saskatchewan, and simultaneously entered politics as a Reciprocity campaigner for Sir Wilfrid Laurier.

He quickly perceived that Providence had designed him for public life, proceeded to conform to this destiny by running for the Saskatchewan legislature in North Qu'Appelle, was elected in June, 1914, and has held the seat ever since.

He has a tenacious pugnacity which knows no dismay, has spent most of his life overcoming difficulties, and now feels that there is something wrong when things are easy.

He introduced himself to federal politics during the war by opposing Union Government in a manner quite consistent with his belief that the party of his allegiance cannot possibly be wrong on any matter of public policy.

He was on the job again at the national Liberal convention of 1919, picked Mr. Mackenzie King as the ultimate winner, and made his preference noticeable at the proper time.

He thinks Mr. King still likes him well enough but would be more comfortable if he felt fully certain of it.

He disclaims any suggestion that he contested the selection of Mr. Dunning as Premier of Saskatchewan in 1922, and it is probably more accurate to state that he favoured it with all the enthusiasm which one would expect a barbers' convention to display in welcoming a safety razor salesman.

One thing about it which he did not disapprove was his own subsequent appointment as Minister of Highways, a position which he filled with such diligence as to give him a prompt and intimate working knowledge of the political machine.

His industry in this respect was rewarded in 1926 when Mr. Dunning went to Ottawa as Minister of Railways and he succeeded to the Premiership, an arrangement which he recognized as an improvement for Saskatchewan anyway.

He is pleased to reflect upon the kind of help he was able to render Mr. Dunning at Ottawa and maintains that good Liberals should always stick together.

He had his first election as party leader in 1929 and was defeated in a campaign against him which he likes to describe as the most outrageous in Canadian political history.

Unflattering references to him since that time are quickly classified by his friends as renewal of the 1929 scurrilities, with the result that a number of Saskatchewan citizens are periodically in danger of apoplectic seizure.

He proved so doughty a combatant in opposition that, when another provincial election came along last June, the Conservatives took care to see that he got into power again.

He has always liked Third Party movements about as well as he likes Tories, has no use for peaceful absorption and, in his present hostility to the C.C.F., may yet succeed in making it an important party in Saskatchewan.

Most of the federal members from Saskatchewan regard him with the circumspection which one is apt to have for a buzz-saw in action.

He has a smile which he hopes will someday be famous.

SIR CHARLES

May, 1933.

SIR CHARLES BLAIR GORDON has been president of the Bank of Montreal since 1928, and hopes that the first five years are the worst.

He has become so accustomed to visitors in trouble that any person of optimistic tendencies is likely to be regarded as an object of suspicion.

He receives visitors in a room equipped with an old-fashioned fireplace and a general atmosphere of pleasant comfort which is sometimes at variance with the episodes enacted therein.

There is never any trouble about getting in to see him provided one has a sufficiently bad debit balance.

He often protects himself by assuming a manner of inattention which he maintains very well until Shawinigan is mentioned, but in moments of responsiveness is able to call upon a vocabulary which is fully adequate.

It is never safe to assume that he is not listening to what is being said.

He feels rather uncomfortable if obliged to reach the Bank before ten-thirty or so, but does not mind working late as long as he has time to drop in at the Mount Royal Club on the way home.

His conversations there occasionally become so engrossing that he continues the discussion at his house and forgets to dine until nine o'clock or later.

Usually he is not particularly noted as a conversationalist unless the subject happens to be the question of how and when a loan should be called.

His greatest talent lies in dissecting financial statements, the common belief being that he can sit in a dark room blindfolded and pick out the jokers in any balance sheet one cares to hand him.

He pretends to be less diplomatic than he really is.

At the Bank he likes to wear a yellow sweater beneath

a double-breasted grey flannel coat, the result being an appearance of informality which has sometimes misled too hopeful strangers.

He was born in Montreal, went through Montreal High School and started to work when he was nineteen.

He will be sixty-six this November (1933) and does not enjoy reminders of it.

His first job was with a wholesale drygoods house called McIntyre, Son and Company at five dollars a month. He was so efficient that his salary was increased to $150 a year before he left.

After five years of this he had saved some money and had observed enough of the stupidities of business to convince him that he could do well on his own, so he organized the Standard Shirt Company.

He nursed this along for three years and confirmed his belief that the chief stupidity was competition. He thereupon proceeded to create Canadian Converters, Limited, which eliminated his competitors by the simple process of bringing them in with him.

He then perceived the wider possibilities which lay in applying the same process to the textile producers. The result was a combination of competing textile mills to form Dominion Textile Company, of which he was installed as vice-president and later as president and managing director.

These ingenuities so excited the admiration and envy of St. James Street that he was invited to become a director of the Bank of Montreal, which shows how an honest manufacturer can be diverted from his purpose.

He is now on the boards of over thirty companies and has even become a governor of Royal Victoria Hospital, a position of virtue which Montreal regards as final proof of a gentleman's eminence.

He is also in the hotel business as president of the Ritz Carlton, an establishment which lately has derived a considerable part of its revenue from distressed industrialists visiting Montreal to see the Bank.

He owns a Scottish castle near the home of his Highland forefathers, and likes to go over there for a holiday in spite of some of his guests.

He regards it as sacrilegious to take it with anything but a little soda, and refuses ice in it.

His house in Montreal is named Terra Nova and is next door to Brother Andre's Shrine. The two establishments are similar in that both of them have visitors seeking mercy.

He keeps five or six dogs at the house and sometimes envies them.

During the War the Government appropriated him for the Imperial Munitions Board, with such gratifying results that the British Government borrowed him in 1917 to go to Washington as Director-General of War Supplies for Great Britain.

He got his knighthood a few months later, partly as a reward for the high effectiveness of his services and partly as a means of dazzling American munitioneers into still more satisfactory responses.

After the War there was a rumour that he was going to be installed at Washington as first Canadian Minister to the United States, but he preferred to keep on working.

His occasional ventures into political strategy have indicated that his choice of these alternatives was wise.

He thoroughly believes in democratic government as long as it does not become a nuisance.

He thinks the newsprint industry could very easily be improved by several applications of dynamite and a few fatal accidents.

Even his strongest critics are obliged to admit that he has come through four years of depression with enhanced reputation as an industrialist although not, perhaps, as a philanthropist.

He is more generous than any genuine Scot should be, but not at the Bank.

MR. GUNDY

July, 1933.

MR. J. H. GUNDY is one reason why so many of our bright young men went into the financial business and are now trying to sell life insurance.

He is short and stocky, with candid grey eyes, fresh red cheeks, round dimpled chin and an engaging air of earnest innocence.

Toronto newspapers used to take local pride in referring to him as the boy millionaire but there is perhaps some question as to whether either of these descriptives would be fully appropriate today.

He was born in Harriston, Ontario, went to school in London and Windsor, and started to work when he was eighteen.

His first job was in Toronto as a clerk in the Central Canada Savings & Loan Company, a highly respectable institution although it had a bond department.

He had this job for two years until the bond department became so vigorous that it had to be separately organized as The Dominion Securities Corporation, and he was made secretary of the new company.

After five years of this he realized that anybody could make money in the bond business, so he started Wood, Gundy & Company for that purpose.

He was twenty-five years old then, is now fifty-three, and in the meantime has proved that his idea was correct.

He kept Wood, Gundy & Company strictly in the government and municipal bond business for fifteen years or so and had a nice, quiet office in the Toronto C. P. R. building, with thick green carpet on the floor and a general atmosphere of conscientious endeavour.

When war broke out he was thirty-four and doing very nicely.

He attracted to his company a number of young men of outstanding ability and still has one or two left.

When his office became too small he moved to the present premises on King Street West, Toronto, where he distributed the young men over a whole ground floor in a suitably financial manner.

He finally decided, however, that the bond business was pretty dull and that it would be more fun to become an investment banker.

To become an investment banker means to get hold of a company with a good name, re-organize it on the right lines, and then get some fellow to run it.

Re-organizing a company on the right lines means to set up several new classes of preferred and common shares and sell these to the public in such a manner that a satisfactory residue remains.

His first escape from dullness was the acquisition and disposal of a small hosiery concern, a deal which turned out so well that he has practically forgotten it.

This was merely a warming-up for the first of his newsprint ventures at Port Alfred. It was here that he first combined with Sir Herbert Holt, an alliance for which one of them at least has entirely lost his earlier enthusiasm.

His attempts at golf have been about as satisfactory as his game of bridge and if he were no better at bonds than he is at bridge he would probably have to go into politics.

He has been a Liberal in politics but, as Sir Herbert used to point out to him, this has never brought him much business.

After Port Alfred he began to demonstrate what an investment banker can really do for the country, with Canada Cement, Besco, Massey-Harris, Simpson's, Canada Power and other re-organizations, each of which brought new gasps of admiration from the Toronto papers.

Of these adventures, Canada Power probably holds the fondest memories because it led to his charming friendship with Mr. Archibald R. Graustein, a resident of New York who is usually to be found at the Ritz-Carlton in Montreal.

He has now returned from investment banking to the

bond business and, in spite of whatever handicaps he may have, he still appears to sell more bonds than any other dealer in Toronto.

During the last couple of years the Canadian Bank of Commerce has become quite keenly interested in his affairs and he now deals with Sir Joseph Flavelle instead of Sir Herbert.

He finds the change rather comfortable because he and Sir Joseph are both possessed of that evangelican emotionalism which distinguishes the really successful Toronto citizen but which merely makes Montreal a little nervous.

His father was a Methodist minister and he is a Methodist by disposition. He went United Church because force of habit made him favour the merger.

He has a Chinese pilgrim's staff which some United Church missionaries gave him in 1929 and prizes this highly because he thinks he may have to use it one of these days.

His young men sometimes refer to him as The Chief and he used to wish that Sir Herbert might overhear them.

He has personality rather than character and a talent in salesmanship which approaches hypnotism.

When upbraided by a disgruntled investor he usually ends by extracting an order for some more bonds.

His personal office is equipped with a telephone booth which he used to use for private conversations when he had visitors, but this has become a little dusty the last couple of years.

He gets more fun out of business than anything else and, even these days, is apt to hang around the office until seven o'clock or so under the delusion that he is working.

He is so determined and persistent that he never gives up hope until the bank says he has to.

Whatever his faults may be, timidity is not one of them.

MR. GUTHRIE

November, 1933.

THE HONOURABLE MR. HUGH GUTHRIE has a straight back, a square jaw, and an amphibious talent for winning elections.

He well demonstrates the practicality of politics as a profession, having succeeded thereby in drawing a comfortable income from the federal treasury for the past thirty-four years.

The loyal citizens of Guelph, Ontario, gave him another public stipend for fifteen years or so as City Solicitor and also as County Solicitor, two positions which his father held before him.

He was obliged to surrender these latter sources of revenue when Mr. Bennett finally made him Minister of Justice in 1930 but undoubtedly feels that honour has its own reward.

Apart from that, he would be glad sometime to become a judge, although he would probably accept a senatorship rather than nothing at all.

Quite a number of people believe that he would make an excellent occupant of Rideau Hall, chiefly because his habits of industry seem peculiarly appropriate to the duties he would thus be called up to perform.

He is sixty-seven years old and works as hard as he ever did.

He was born in Guelph, a city famous for stone houses, Presbyterians, Mr. Edward Johnson, who sings tenor in New York, and Mr. Arthur Cutten who talks money in Chicago.

He greatly admires Mr. Johnson's genius but has had more use for Mr. Cutten's.

He attended Guelph Collegiate and then took law at Osgoode Hall, but has never allowed this to interfere with his career.

He entered politics in 1899, was a Liberal for eighteen years, became a Unionist for a necessary interval, and has

63

been a Conservative since the war, a sequence which Mr. Woodsworth would probably describe as going from bad to worse.

Regardless of his variations in party affiliation, South Wellington has never failed to elect him and he has commanded the allegiance of Guelph's citizens to a degree which is only partly explained by the hours he has spent trudging the city's streets in house-to-house canvassing.

As an orator he is splendid to look at.

He was a highly decorative feature of Sir Wilfrid Laurier's front benches and was about to succeed Sir Allan Aylesworth as Minister of Justice when the Liberals were so inconsiderate as to lose the Reciprocity campaign and that cabinet chance went glimmering.

His next chance was in 1917 when he distinguished himself by being the first of the front-benchers to leave Sir Wilfrid. He was thereupon taken into the Unionist cabinet as Solicitor-General, a supernumary office the duties of which have always been a trifle obscure to the average tax-payer.

His parliamentary deportment has always been perfect and includes the fortunate faculty of looking more distinguished that he really is.

In 1920, the war being over, Mr. Arthur Meighen appointed him Minister of Defence, which shows that a lawyer in politics can be almost anything as long as there is not much to do.

As Minister of Defence he attempted to direct the Inspector-Generalship of Sir Arthur Currie until the latter resigned in disgust to hibernate at McGill, an institution of learning which still hopes to have a fooball team again sometime.

He quite enjoyed being Minister of Defence, however, and went into the 1921 election as a Conservative, adopting at that time the quip with which he has ever since answered his critics, that anybody was welcome to his discarded opinions.

He survived the Conservative slaughter of 1921 just as he had escaped the Liberal massacre of 1911, which shows how South Wellington can be inspired to rise above mere partisanship when a citizen's livelihood is at stake.

He used to play a little cricket and still plays a little golf but his chief diversions are sedentary.

He pretty well succeeded in establishing himself as a genuine Conservative during the tribulations which followed 1921, but was as surprised as anybody else when he was chosen temporary leader of the party upon Mr. Meighen's elevation to investment banking in 1926.

He had the further distinction of acting as Chairman of the party's convention at Winnipeg in 1927 and performed this duty very well indeed, except for a slight mental reversion when he opened proceedings by calling "this National Liberal convention" to order.

He came second to Mr. Bennett in the vote for leader, this being the only election on record which he has ever lost.

Following the 1930 election he had a trip to the Imperial Conference and completed this just in time to manage the details of his daughter's marriage to Captain Victor Blundell Hollinshead Blundell, one of Lord Willingdon's aides-de-camp.

On this occasion he delivered an oration in which he referred to Lady Willingdon in such complimentary fashion that she interrupted his remarks by embracing him, which probably served him right.

He had another trip to Geneva in 1931 as Canadian representative at the League of Nations, and is beginning to feel that he is about due for another holiday.

He strongly opposed purchase of the Washington legation but, like other Conservative statesmen, is now charmed to think of its being occupied by a brilliant young man like Mr. Herridge.

He hopes to see Mr. Herridge go a long way.

MR. HEPBURN

August, 1934.

MR. HORATIO ALGER HEPBURN is the youngest Premier Ontario has ever had and is getting sick of hearing it.

His proper names are Mitchell Frederick, but nine people out of ten refer to him as Mitch and the tenth person calls him Hep.

To some of the Liberal bigwigs he has thus represented an informality so distressing that they kept carefully aloof from his campaign efforts and he was obliged to win without them.

Some of them are still reluctant to rejoice because they fear that he will continue to disregard their counsel and consequently wreck the party.

He is soft-hearted and hard-headed.

He will probably do a good deal of public laundry work during the next few months as he believes that the Ontario cupboard contains several items of soiled linen needing sun and air.

In this he will have the ready assistance of Mr. Arthur G. Slaght, K. C., a perspicacious gentleman who has manifested considerable interest in the clothes hamper left behind by Mr. G. Howard Ferguson.

He will also, if not careful, have assistance from other reformers whose conception of social progress is Sunday movies and free beer.

He was born and still lives on a farm near St. Thomas, Ontario, where his father and grandfather lived before him. His great-grandfather was one of the adherents of a man named William Lyon Mackenzie in 1837.

The farm has six hundred acres, six silos and a black dog and supports over thirty people, including workers and their families.

He went to the township public school and then used to drive in every day to St. Thomas Collegiate with the idea that he would eventually become a lawyer.

His education ended abruptly, however, a few weeks before matriculation, following a Hydro meeting when he was wrongly accused of throwing an apple which knocked off Sir Adam Beck's hard hat.

He declined to apologize for something he had not done, walked out of the collegiate and got a job as clerk in the Bank of Commerce down the street.

His grandfather persuaded him to carry on the farm but it was agreed that a while in business might be useful, so he stayed with the bank for two years, was sent out to the Winnipeg main office and promoted to cashier at seventeen.

He had his thirty-eighth birthday in August (1934) and thus was still seventeen when war broke out twenty years ago.

He advanced his birthday the necessary few days in 1914 in order to join the Fort Garry Horse without delay, but his family had him discharged as under age and kept him home for a couple of years.

Then he joined the Air Force and was in training when he had an automobile accident which put him into hospital for six months and finished his military endeavours.

The injuries suffered in this accident became apparent later in the form of a recalcitrant kidney which he was obliged to have removed in the summer of 1931.

His health since then has been so delicate that he cannot get along with much less than three or four hours' sleep a night and he begins to feel weary if he has more than six speeches to make in a day.

To make a speech he merely turns on the tap and releases an unfailing flow of barbed-wire eloquence which even Dr. Manion, the gatling-gun from Fort William, cannot match in rapidity and certainly not in deadliness.

He got into politics immediately after the war, when he helped to start the United Farmer organization in East Elgin. His first election was in 1926 when he came off the farm to win a riding which had not elected a Liberal since 1891.

During his first session at Ottawa he displayed certain symptoms of bumptiousness which caused many observers to conclude that he was merely another of the Boy Wonders who periodically reach Ottawa and soon disappear.

He discovered his mistakes in time, started in to study public questions and within a couple of years had made a place for himself as one of the best catch-as-catch-can exponents in the Commons.

He is fortunate in his equipment of courage, buoyancy and industry and has the priceless political gift of being able to disagree without quarrelling.

At his next federal election in the summer of 1930, despite a Conservative landslide, he managed to win Elgin West again with an increased majority.

Six months later he was shanghaied into taking the Ontario leadership, partly because the Liberal moguls couldn't think of anyone else and partly because some of them felt it didn't matter much anyway.

His mode of living in the three and a half years since then would drive any doctor to despair, but he has managed to revive himself at intervals by escaping to the farm for a couple of days' hard work.

On his campaign visits to Toronto the number of his room at the King Edward was always kept a secret, with such complete success that he was sometimes there for ten or fifteen minutes before the room was jammed with people who had the idea that he never ate nor slept.

He now lives in an apartment at the King Edward and has a strictly private telephone number which not more than several thousand friends have discovered.

His greatest asset is his ability to make people like him and his chief danger consists in his friends.

A number of people have deprecated his propensity to wisecracking, including Mr. Henry.

MR. HERRIDGE

October, 1933.

MR. WILLIAM DUNCAN HERRIDGE is a public skyrocket touched off by Mr. Bennett in 1930 and still travelling so fast that several watchful waiters have almost abandoned hope of seeing the descent.

He is at present Canadian Minister at Washington and lives there whenever he can get away from helping to run things at Ottawa.

He has had more to do with governing the country during the last three years than anyone except Mr. Bennett, and is probably the closest approach to a phenomenon in Canadian politics.

At forty-seven, he is still a clever young man.

He is also highly likeable and has always enjoyed unusual success in winning the esteem of older notables.

He was born and educated in Ottawa and then went to Toronto University. At Varsity he hurt his back playing football and was laid up for two years but managed to graduate in 1909 as a classmate of Mr. Vincent Massey, the Port Hope hopeful.

After that he went through Osgoode Hall, joined a legal firm in Ottawa, and was in some danger of becoming a successful lawyer when the war came.

His father and both of his grandfathers were ministers but his behaviour has always been quite respectable.

He entered an officers' training course in Toronto in November, 1914, secured his commission, and then paid his own way to England under the delusion that he had better hurry if he wanted to reach France before everything was over.

He got to France in the summer of 1915 as a cavalryman, was transferred to divisional cyclists, became a staff officer and ended up as Acting Captain and brigade-major with D.S.O., M.C. and bar, two mentions in despatches and a surprisingly close friendship with Lord Byng.

71

He has a house in Ottawa and a country place in the Gatineau hills where he likes to get into the woods by himself and chop down trees.

He is a perfect host when he feels like it.

After he got out of the army he became interested in public questions of the day and formed an association of local discussion groups called the Canadian League.

Although he insists that he had no political affiliations at this time he was regarded as a Liberal, two of his best friends being Mr. Mackenzie King and the old classmate, Mr. Vincent Massey.

He was, however, a still warmer friend of Lord Byng (then Governor-General) and the beautiful friendship with Mr. King came to a sudden stop in the summer of 1926 when the constitutional dispute arose.

His chumminess with Mr. Massey began to wear a bit thin too and is now invisible.

He gradually became a reasonably eminent Ottawa lawyer, specializing in patent cases. He took several of these to the Privy Council but was scarcely regarded as a legal genius until Mr. Bennett said so.

His acquaintance with Mr. Bennett began in the spring of 1930 when they travelled together from Ottawa to Montreal to attend a funeral and discussed affairs of state.

He impressed Mr. Bennett at once as a great mind and by the time the train reached Montreal the Right Honourable gentleman was enthralled.

A simple explanation of this sudden triumph is that his intelligence was a startling change from the mentalities with whom Mr. Bennett had hitherto been obliged to confer.

When the 1930 election came along a few weeks later he toured the country as Mr. Bennett's Chief-of-Staff, helped to formulate the Canada First policy, wrote speeches and pretty well ran the Conservative show.

After the victory he was described by Mr. Bennett as the man who had made him Prime Minister, and was taken

72

over to the Imperial Conference to keep some of the new cabinet ministers and other small fry out of the way.

To the Conservative Old Guard, who had wandered in the wilderness these many years, all this was like sprinkling paris green on the milk and honey.

It was, however, quite innocuous compared with the Tory tortures which ensued when the young man came back from London to carry off the prize of the Washington Legation and then climaxed this performance by wedding the Prime Minister's sister, a person so thoroughly nice that even the Toronto *Telegram* is obliged to like her.

The moanings of various Conservative newspapers when he was sent to Washington were most distressing. Apparently these journals felt that the appointment should go to one of the numerous intellectuals among the Tried and True, or to a Worthy Senator.

(A Worthy Senator is an elderly gentleman with liver trouble, who has never voted wrong and always donated right.)

His performance at Washington has been so capable that there is not much a critic can say, but the Old Guard are still unhappy and if they ever get a chance they will pull him down as quickly as he was pushed up.

It is doubtful if he would mind, for he has ability but not ambition.

In his first ten months at Washington he made twenty-eight trips to Ottawa and spent more time there than at the Legation. One reason for this was Mrs. Herridge's residence at Chateau Laurier prior to the arrival of a son and heir in April, 1932.

He is delightfully amiable and entertaining at times but occasionally indulges in black moods when he is irritable, silent and completely unpleasant.

He rates, however, as an excellent mixer and talks almost too well.

He may end up as a man without a party but in the meantime he hardly needs one.

MR. HOUDE

June, 1934.

MR. CAMILLIEN HOUDE is a political Lazarus who finds that being mayor of Montreal is simpler than trying to sell insurance.

As a political figure he was regarded as being permanently interred two years ago and only a few months ago had been reduced by pressure of economic forces to a point where comfortable existence was a matter of some concern.

This spring he suddenly emerged with a dazzling wardrobe, a flourishing embonpoint and the largest majority Montreal has ever bestowed upon a mayoralty candidate.

His campaign advisors included a group of public-spirited gentlemen who were willing to exert themselves entirely for the good of the common people.

No one in Montreal suspects that these gentlemen will now attempt to exert any influence upon the course of civic affairs except when their public spirit is aroused again.

He will be forty-five this summer, has twice previously been mayor of Montreal, had seven years or so in the Provincial Legislature, and created quite a stir as leader of the Quebec Conservatives until Mr. Taschereau became annoyed and burst the bubble in 1931.

He intends now to be leader of a new political party by which he hopes to rescue the province from despotism, just as soon as he has found time to get Montreal out of bankruptcy.

He is five feet six inches tall, weighs 220 pounds, has his hair slicked down, and smokes large Turkish cigarettes which he likes to hand around to people.

He possesses what the newspapers describe as a compelling personality, and during his previous terms of office twice managed to make public appearances in Toronto without being censored.

He likes to wear double-breasted blue suits, spats, bright

yellow gloves and malacca stick and on this account is quite pleased to be back at the City Hall.

Several policemen guard his City Hall office with suitable ceremony, but his practice has been to conduct affairs of state from the more comfortable confusion of a suite at the Place Viger Hotel.

He stopped going to school when he was sixteen, got a job with the Bank of Hochelaga, became a branch manager at twenty-six, and soon after was the youngest bank inspector in the province.

Thus perceiving the simplicity of success, he started a candy business, but when this proved more difficult than banking he resorted to selling insurance, which is still his official occupation.

He could speak no English until he was twenty-three or so, but can now orate in either English or French with hypnotic effect.

He found insurance almost as bad as the bank and, when the provincial election of 1923 came along, he thought he might as well try politics. There was a Liberal candidate already nominated in his riding so he decided to be a Conservative.

He got the Conservative nomination in St. Mary's because nobody else wanted it and then won the election because nobody thought he had a chance.

At the next election in 1927 the Liberal strategists were not so careless and gave him a trimming but he raised such a rumpus that the new Liberal member resigned and there was a by-election.

He found himself a little short of funds while waiting for this by-election so he ran for mayor of Montreal in the spring of 1928, beat Mr. Mederic Martin and picked up a $10,000 salary.

Then he won the by-election, went to Quebec and a few months later was made leader of the Conservative party. He was not quite forty at the time, but modestly refrained from mentioning his youth to anybody except newspaper reporters.

He was elected mayor of Montreal again in 1930 and was so busy that he hardly noticed it.

He intended to become Premier of Quebec in the provincial election of 1931 but neglected to get enough votes. By the summer of 1932, instead of being mayor and premier, he was merely an insurance salesman again.

He has not been heard of since until this April (1934) when he appeared on the scene again as candidate for mayor, made several speeches every day for a couple of weeks and won an election in which all three of his opponents lost their deposits.

He once took a course in elocution with a view to going upon the stage and has never completely recovered from the effects.

He now thinks it improbable that he will ever equal Mr. Meighen's record of becoming Prime Minister of Canada at forty-six, but hopes he will not have to become a senator before he is sixty.

He has never bored anybody, even about insurance.

He is so highly energetic that he is reported to be able to read a newspaper, dictate letters, sing a song, eat breakfast and take a bath all at one time.

He has been twice married, with the unique accomplishment that both his mothers-in-law have been among his most devoted political supporters.

He has a talent for making people angry and also for making them laugh, both abilities being highly useful in the art of statesmanship as practised in Quebec.

He has maintained that he is not at all proud of his achievements because he realizes himself to be a man of destiny, a point of view which has other exponents among his political contemporaries.

MR. KILLAM

April, 1933.

MR. I. W. KILLAM lives in Montreal and is a perfect example of what was once known as the financial magnate, a species rendered almost extinct by the glacial action of frozen assets.

He has a power company in Calgary, a chocolate concern in Halifax, a newsprint enterprise at Liverpool, Nova Scotia, and a good deal of trouble with all of them.

He also owns a newspaper in Toronto called the *Mail and Empire,* and has hoped some day to own the *Globe* as well.

A great many people have wondered why in the world he bought the *Mail and Empire* and are even more puzzled as to what a man would do with two newspapers, especially two Toronto newspapers.

Such people fail to appreciate the passion of a financier for a merger which often consists of putting together two mistakes and thus making a bigger one.

Another of his activities is a training school for young bond salesmen known as The Royal Securities Corporation, which has one classroom in Montreal, another in Toronto, and a hopeful spirit among the students.

After he has made a visit to the Toronto office all his bright young men feel able to tell the boys what is going to happen to the world for the next week or so.

One of his brightest students in Montreal used to be Mr. Ward Pitfield, who completed his course of training in 1928, started a company of his own, and is now recognized as quite a polo player.

He still values Mr. Pitfield's financial judgment very highly, as long as it coincides with his own.

He lives in a rather ugly brick house on Sherbrooke Street, next door to Lord Atholstan who owns the *Montreal Star,* and, through the generosity of Mr. J. W. McConnell, has demonstrated for several years that it is quite possible to have your cake and eat it too.

Among his other near neighbours is Sir Herbert Holt, the famous Santa Claus non-impersonator.

He does not sleep very well, and blames this on the traffic along Sherbrooke Street except when he is thinking of selling the house.

He has three telephone numbers at his house, one for himself, one for the servants and one for his garage, and could easily get along without the first of these, since he rarely speaks on the telephone unless caught unawares.

He does not speak at all unless he has to.

He would rather go around and call on a man than telephone, and would sooner have nothing to do with him than write a letter.

He makes a charming tea guest because he can be parked in a corner and will stay there for a couple of hours without saying anything, especially since the Fall of '29.

When he bought the *Mail and Empire* he induced Mr. John Scott to forsake a well-established job printing business in Montreal, publicly known as the *Gazette*, in order to let Toronto see how a newspaper should be conducted, the result to date being of greater benefit to Toronto than to Mr. Scott.

He is usually not as tired as he looks.

His office in Montreal is on St. James Street, a capitalistic thoroughfare inhabited by some distressing cases of arrested mental development and at present in a state of suspended animation.

He was born in Yarmouth, Nova Scotia, sold papers until he was seventeen, and then got a job in a bank, which at that time was regarded as an upward step.

He got out of the bank three years later when Lord Beaverbrook, a permanent adolescent as modest then as now, undertook to show Canada some new altitudes of finance and started Royal Securities as one instrument of the demonstration.

He was pleased to acquire the Royal Securities business when Lord Beaverbrook, having outgrown this country, went over to help England realize that the age of chivalry is past.

He seldom sees Lord Beaverbrook now except when the latter comes back here on some philanthropic mission, such as saving Price Brothers and Company for the sake of the boys.

He has made several million dollars since he left the bank and several years ago was told that he had the smartest financial brain in Canada, a remark which some investors now would be unkind enough to regard as the perfect example of an empty compliment.

He is nearly fifty, wears blue suits, carries a yellow stick, and has romantic brown eyes and a complexion that makes him look slightly in need of a shave.

He made a strict rule some years ago not to be interviewed or photographed by the press and has had little difficulty about this recently.

He is tall, slim, languid and mournful, and is called Ike because his first name is Isaac. His second name is Walton but this is entirely without piscatorial significance.

He may occasionally be observed sitting sadly with a cocktail in the St. James's Club, a business crèche located on Dorchester Street and frequented by a number of gentlemen who have nowhere else to go.

He sometimes goes to a hockey game and now and then to a theatre, at both of which he displays all the enthusiastic interest of a blind man in an art gallery.

In spite of the inconvenience which frequently results, he is disposed by nature to be friendly with people.

He is even quite friendly with Lord Beaverbrook although he has known him ever since they were bank clerks together in Halifax thirty years ago.

MR. KING

August, 1934.

MR. W. L. MACKENZIE KING went to school for twenty years and then became a statesman, which shows the futility of higher learning.

He does not mind being Leader of the Opposition because it gives him more time to work on his memoirs.

He would, however, like to have a few more years as Prime Minister in order to give the book a happier ending and intends to manage this as soon as he is sure the depression is over.

With the approach of this possibility, he is becoming increasingly popular with a number of watchful gentlemen, and tries to think that they love him for himself alone.

He was born in Kitchener, Ontario, and was there first elected to the House of Commons when he was thirty-four years old.

He will be sixty in December (1934) but does not expect many roses from the Byngs.

His father was John King and his mother was the daughter of Mr. William Lyon Mackenzie, a historic gentleman whose disagreement with despotism now permits every farmer between Hamilton and Toronto to show tourists the very cave in which he once sought refuge.

He has never hidden in a cave himself but probably would have been glad to find one during his accidental venture into the Valley of Humiliation.

This venture brought pleasure to various observers, but it is never safe for opponents to rejoice too fully in his misfortune for he is at his best when stimulated by adversity. He is at his worst when matters are too easy.

Most of his best speeches to date have been those delivered with an emotional spontaneity born of necessity, and his poorest have usually been the most elaborately prepared.

He does not enjoy being grateful to people.

He went through University of Toronto with a thoroughness which made him a bachelor of arts in 1895, a bachelor of laws in 1896, and a master of arts in 1897. To play safe, he became a Harvard master of arts in 1898.

He then felt sufficiently educated to become a reporter on the Toronto *Globe*, made himself known as an expert on labour problems and acquired a Napoleonic conception of his destiny.

This was considerably assisted when his friend, Sir William Mulock, made him Deputy Minister of Labour at twenty-six and spoke well of him to Sir Wilfrid.

As Deputy Minister he toiled with suitable diligence for eight years, then got himself elected to parliament and became Minister of Labour, which meant that he did not have to work so hard.

He has a hearty laugh, but hardly a proportionate sense of humour.

He had only two years as Minister of Labour because he was defeated in the 1911 election. He was defeated again in 1917, but remained aware of his destiny and was less surprised than gratified when he was chosen Leader of the Liberal party at the national convention in 1919.

Two years later he was Prime Minister, which shows that the main thing in politics is to win at the right time.

He dislikes being bothered by people who want things done.

Although he won only one election as Prime Minister he stayed in power from 1921 until 1930, with the exception of an interval in the summer of 1926 which was just long enough for Mr. Meighen to discover how wrong a Board of Strategy can be.

He has always felt quite friendly toward Mr. Meighen, perhaps because he has always beaten him.

He has a tendency to procrastinate until a crisis is upon him and he then improvises under fire with a skill which sometimes has transported his followers from desperation to delight.

He has always enjoyed attending an Imperial Conference, this being an opportunity to replenish his wardrobe with both economy and decorum.

He is possessed of a Canadianism appropriate to his ancestry and is invariably aroused to an effectively righteous indignation by anything which he can interpret as a reactionary restriction of constitutional rights.

He has a genius for detecting the approach of trouble and an equal talent for avoiding it.

He rarely does any table-pounding but has never failed to maintain firm control of his cabinets even when they contained such oil and water mixtures as Mr. Dunning and Mr. Euler.

His technique in handling difficult situations ranges from urbane persuasion to indignant protestation, either of which he employs with practised artistry.

His persistent celibacy has given him extreme proficiency in details of household overhead which he watches with the zeal of a boarding-house landlady. No crisis in parliament has ever made him entirely unmindful of the laundry bill.

To visitors at Laurier House he is a solicitous and generous host and takes a justifiable pride in his top floor library, where he would spend all his time if he did not have to bother about his career.

He likes to work there on his diary, which he occasionally shows to persons believed capable of appreciating it.

He has another place in the country at Kingsmere, admires its sheep and other facilities and is glad that parliament does not sit all summer.

Reports of his ill-health in recent months have had no visible support beyond the loss of considerable weight, which the Liberal caucus regards as an improvement.

He has preserved his academic instinct, has sometimes thought with longing of a Chair at Oxford, and may yet crown his career with the pleasurable dignity which a university can bestow.

MR. LAPOINTE

December, 1933.

MR. ERNEST LAPOINTE has become the most influential figure in the Liberal party, but does not allow anyone to say so.

In Quebec he holds the affection which belonged to Laurier and in the west his new prestige now mounts so high that he might win surprising support in a Liberal convention.

He sees no need, however, for a party convention and bestows upon Mr. Mackenzie King an oral, visual and auricular fidelity closely resembling that displayed by the image of the three monkeys.

As long as this continues it is quite impossible for any malcontent gentlemen within the party to accomplish the dethronement which they sometimes like to talk about.

He entered politics four years before Mr. King but is not yet, and probably never will be, a practical politician in the sense which many of his contemporaries understand.

He is, for example, quite useless in campaign fund skull-duggery and has little talent in other similar essentials of democratic government.

He does not even appreciate such talent among his associates, who occasionally try to do a little fence-mending on his behalf, and has gone so far as to suspect them of tampering with the electorate which is, of course, quite unthinkable in any Quebec constituency.

He was born on a habitant farm at St. Eloi, a typical little tin-spired Quebec village on the St. Lawrence below Rivière du Loup, and was brought up with the prospect of continuing to till the few acres his father had cleared.

He belongs to the seventh generation of his family in Quebec but can hardly expect to be regarded as a genuine Canadian by a certain type of citizen west of the Ottawa River.

His career as a farmer was cancelled by his parish priest

who sent him to college at Rimouski as good material for the Church.

At Rimouski, however, he won a scholarship which sent him on to Laval University for law and, instead of becoming either a farmer or a priest, he eventually began as a young lawyer in Fraserville.

He was a huge young man and, to his six feet three, has gradually added a girth and general bulk which make him today the largest physical specimen in the House of Commons.

In Fraserville he became a friend of the Crown Prosecutor, an enterprising gentleman named Carroll, who later entered politics as the member for Kamouraska.

He got into politics himself when his friend Carroll moved up to a judgeship and presented him with the vacant seat in parliament which he duly won at a by-election in 1904.

He squared matters with Mr. Carroll twenty-five years later by assisting him to his eminence as Lieutenant-Governor of Quebec.

When he succeeded Mr. Carroll at Ottawa in 1904 he could neither read nor speak English and, in many respects, seemed almost as ill-equipped for public life as certain members of the present cabinet.

He occasionally attempted to address the House in French but, whenever aroused, was seized by such ungovernable rage that he usually became inarticulate within a few minutes.

He sat in obscurity on the back benches year after year and might still be there if Jacques Bureau, the late tactician from Three Rivers, had not persuaded him to learn English.

He accomplished this by memorizing lists of English words, which his friend Bureau used to give him every morning, and by sticking to a promise that he would speak no French for an entire session of parliament.

He made his first English speech in the House at the next session in 1913, moved up to the front bench four years later, and there suddenly emerged as an eloquent and courageous combatant who more than filled the place left vacant by that great defender of high principle, Mr. Hugh Guthrie.

He now speaks English better than Mr. Guthrie and more often.

He used to wear a small beret in the House but abandoned it when he reached the front bench, although the beret might have become as famous as the yellow sweater which Sir Charles Gordon has made familiar.

When he wore the beret he had nice, thick, curly auburn hair but now has the complete baldness appropriate to a Liberal under the present regime.

He employs a naive and innocent manner, which it is highly dangerous to accept too literally.

He has several times represented Canada in London, Paris and Geneva, and will now argue with passion that Europe has no scenery to equal his Laurentians and the valley of the St. Lawrence.

One of the pearls he has frequently tossed to the electors is that a Liberal is a Liberal because he loves something and a Tory is a Tory because he hates something.

In 1927 the Alliance Francaise gave him an all-French dinner in Toronto which was probably one of the greatest nervous shocks that city has ever survived.

He is honest to the point of being quixotic and so instinctively loyal to established authority that he is almost able to defer today to some of the Honourable gentlemen who handicap Mr. Bennett.

He also defers a little to Miss Agnes Macphail because he has found this to be safer.

He used to describe Mr. Meighen as being great in small things and small in great things but has not yet found a public epigram to fit Mr. Taschereau.

He has always felt grateful to the Conservative Board of Strategy and hopes there will be one in the next election.

He still thinks the habitant farmers are the backbone of the country and likes to believe that he is one of them.

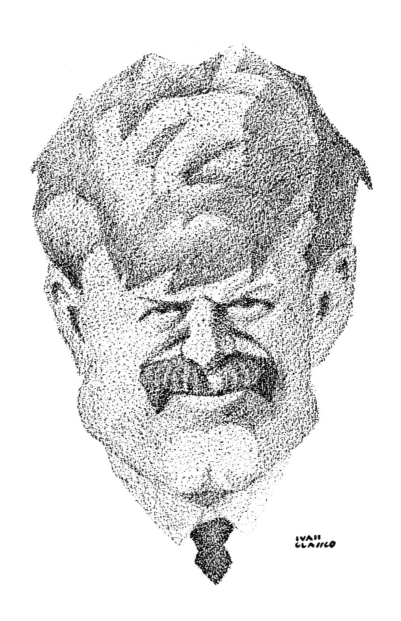

MR. LEACOCK

August, 1934.

MR. STEPHEN BUTLER LEACOCK is an intellectual acrobat who lives in Montreal and is officially known as head of the Department of Economics at McGill University.

He has been a humourist by endowment, an economist by environment, and a radio performer by mistake.

When he lectures on economics he is glad he is a humourist and, when now obliged to write something funny, he is thankful to be a professor.

As an economist he started with five hundred dollars a year from McGill and now receives about six thousand. As a humourist he has made up to fifty thousand or so a year but has successfully avoided accumulation of undue wealth by applying both economics and humour to the stock market.

In his stock market operations he is always bullish on distillery shares, his attitude being based upon an exaggerated estimate of per capita consumption.

He was born in England, came to Canada with his family when he was seven and settled near Lake Simcoe, Ontario, on a farm which proved so unprofitable that he was forced to seek education as a preliminary to livelihood.

He was sent to Upper Canada College and University of Toronto and finished this programme when he was twenty-two with an arts degree in classics, an extensive experience of boarding houses and a complete lack of any commercially useful knowledge.

He thereupon returned to Upper Canada as a master, an occupation which he has since pronounced to be the dreariest, most thankless and worst paid in the world.

He stuck at this for eight years because he could think of nothing else to do but finally, when he was thirty, borrowed enough money to keep him alive for a few months and went to the University of Chicago to study economics and political science.

He won a fellowship at Chicago, got some temporary employment from McGill, and finished four years later as a Doctor of Philosophy, a degree which he explains as meaning that he was so full of education as to preclude his ever holding a new idea on anything.

He was rewarded by being appointed to the regular staff of McGill in 1903 as a lecturer in political science and is since supposed by some to have become an economist.

He will be sixty-five this December (1934) and still lectures at McGill when he can spare the time.

He lives in a red brick house on Cote des Neiges Road in Montreal but greatly prefers his summer place near Orillia, Ontario, which is not inappropriately known as Old Brewery Bay.

He began his humorous writing by way of relief when he was master at Upper Canada and received two dollars for his first sketch. His first book, called *Literary Lapses,* did not appear until fifteen years later.

Apart from humour, he has written a number of economic and historical works. Several people have read these and describe them as models of literary clarity.

He believes that humorous and imaginative writing is far more difficult to do than scientific treatises and has frequently been annoyed by admirers who suppose that he can dash off something funny while taking a bath.

He has no use for typewriters, mechanical or feminine, and does all his writing by long hand in a series of unique hieroglyphics which become decipherable only through patience and experience.

There are many people who consider that his moving tribute to Sir Arthur Currie last December is the finest thing he has ever written.

He is usually up very early in the morning and does his writing between then and eleven o'clock. When he has lectures they are almost always in the afternoon by which time he endeavours to have himself in a suitable frame of mind.

Before proceeding to a lecture he often goes to the trouble of enquiring what the subject is supposed to be, and then equips himself with a moth-eaten set of notes to which he rarely pays any attention.

He occasionally pauses part way through a lecture to remind the students that he has now given them all their fees entitle them to and is delivering the remainder entirely from the goodness of his heart.

He is not wholly unaware that he is one of the few colourful personalities this country has and it may properly be suspected that he is not as absent-minded as he sometimes appears to be.

He is not absent-minded at all when people owe him money.

He is usually finished at McGill by four o'clock and proceeds forthwith to find respite at the University Club, where he likes to start with a game of billards.

He can digest a book by looking at the table of contents and sniffing a couple of pages and can quote chapter, page and text of books he has read in this manner years before.

His clothes are cut on consistently generous lines and are used entirely for utilitarian purposes. He once went out for the evening with the waistcoat of a grey tweed suit beneath his dinner coat and was quite perplexed by the ensuing agitation.

He has worn the same hat for a number of years and has a coonskin coat for which several museums have been scouting with eager, but thus far futile, hope.

He regards barbers, manicurists and neckties as superfluities.

He has a depth of human understanding which none of his mannerisms can conceal and a courage which makes no mention of the sorrows of his own life.

He is always kind to young persons of intellectual ability and never tells them that he has found this qualification to be of minor importance.

GENERAL MACBRIEN

April, 1933.

MAJOR-GENERAL JAMES HOWDEN MACBRIEN, C.B., C.M.G., D.S.O., lives on a farm near Ottawa, eats apples for lunch, has six children, and is one of the three best-looking men in Canada.

He is also head of the Royal Canadian Mounted Police and is probably the most complete soldier this country has produced.

As a method of keeping fit, he frequently occupies the noon hour by swimming in the Chateau Laurier pool, with disturbing effect upon certain other inmates who are merely striving to rouse themselves for another day.

His father was an Irishman from Eniskillen and his mother was Julia Madden of Port Perry, Ontario. They raised the General on a farm near Port Perry and agreed that he should go to college and become a school teacher.

The General, however, made a slight alteration in this arrangement by running away at the age of eighteen and joining the 34th Regiment as a private.

He joined just in time for the South African war, went along in 1900 with a detachment of the Mounties and got the Queen's Medal with five clasps.

When the war was over he stayed out there as a sergeant in the new South African Constabulary, but came back to Canada after four years of it and got his commission as a subaltern in the Royal Canadian Dragoons.

He has never been able to go in much for clubs but has been president of the United Services in Montreal, a strictly teetotal institution on Sherbrooke Street next door to the Mount Royal Club, and sometimes referred to by the more moribund members of the latter as The Little Scorpions' Club.

He was twenty-nine when he got his commission in the Dragoons so he got married as well and was promptly

95

shipped to Australia for two years in an exchange of officers.

His activities in Australia included the introduction of an after-dinner amusement known as cockfighting, this being a form of wrestling in which the combatant gentlemen assume recumbent positions on the floor, lock arms and endeavour to upset each other by using their legs as levers.

At this pastime he was acknowledged to be the undefeated champion of the Antipodes and is still so proficient that he would probably be champion of the Ottawa Valley today if it were not for one named MacDowell, who, in spite of an inherent diffidence of manner, has a habit of being obstinate about such matters.

It is this Colonel MacDowell whose Victoria Cross episode at Vimy the General has described as the finest individual exploit of the war.

The General's office as Commissioner of the Royal Canadian Mounted is over a grocery store on Rideau Street in Ottawa, the location being a matter of continued governmental peculiarity rather than personal preference.

When the war began he was in England taking a staff officers' course and was requisitioned by the War Office to help with mobilization.

As soon as the First Canadian Contingent reached England he was appointed to the staff as major, went to France, spent far too much time in the front line to be a proper staff officer, and so was made brigadier-general of the 12th Brigade in 1916.

Even this, however, failed to suppress his reprehensible habit of prowling around the front line with a sniper's rifle, in which respect he established an all-time record for brigadier-generals.

His official score for the war included two wounds, six mentions in dispatches, a D.S.O. and bar, a C.B., a C.M.G. and a Legion of Honour.

He thinks the Canadians' hardest battle was Passchendaele; the most deadly weapon, mustard gas; the most dangerous rank, a junior infantry officer.

He knows it is risky for a soldier to be clever but once ventured the epigrammatical profundity that security without peace is better than peace without security.

After the armistice he became a major-general and was kept in England for a year looking after Canadian demobilization.

By the time he got back to Canada in 1920 Sir Arthur Currie had had enough of cabinet ministers so the general succeeded him as Chief of Staff, the highest military office Miss Agnes Macphail has permitted the country to have.

He worked hard at this and liked it very well indeed except the salary, which finally obliged him to resign in 1927 in favour of civil aviation.

In this new endeavour he acquired a Moth plane from one of the oil companies and piloted himself into every corner of the country. He also engaged in various mergers, became general manager of International Airways of Canada and president of the Aviation League.

These efforts continued until the middle of 1931, when he was made Commissioner of the Mounted, and it is probable that he is better off at this than dealing with boards of directors and other deficients.

He is quite certain there will be another war and, if he were a young man in the next one, would like to be an air-fighter.

He will be fifty-five this summer (1933), was a soldier for thirty-one years, and is privately a little reluctant to realize that he is now a policeman.

No debutante who has seen him in his full dress uniform has ever since been quite the same.

MR. MACKLIN

July, 1934.

MR. E. H. MACKLIN is President of the Winnipeg *Free Press* and sometimes reads it when he is not too busy.

He is probably the most sagacious newspaper publisher in Canada with the exception of Mr. Joseph E. Atkinson who owns the Toronto *Star,* a journal of such versatility that it can give its readers the Work of Charles Dickens and Tillie the Toiler with equal aplomb.

He surpasses Mr. Atkinson, however, in certain other respects, including the possession of a pyrotechnical vocabulary which combines ingenuity and imagination with notable effect.

He is five feet six inches tall, has a white Vandyke beard with moustache to match, and wears wing collars, bow ties and silky black fedora hats. He imports the hats from Italy at great expense and has, on appropriate occasion, presented them to worthy persons as tokens of his great esteem.

He realizes that consistency is often a disguise for stupidity and avoids it with such complete success that nobody who works with him ever knows what he will do next.

His first job in the newspaper business was addressing envelopes and he was so good at this that he became cashier of *The Globe,* a newspaper in Toronto noted for the fortitude with which it endures its local contemporaries.

He stayed with *The Globe* for twenty years and might have been promoted if he had waited a while.

He was in the next room at *The Globe* when George Brown was assassinated which is now so long ago that he does not mention it.

He was invited to Winnipeg by Sir Clifford Sifton in 1899 for the purpose of looking over the *Free Press.* He spent three days in this examination, said that the paper looked pretty bad and thereupon took the job of Business Manager.

He has been there ever since and is beginning to like it.

His eminent partner in the *Free Press* is Mr. John W. Dafoe, his exact opposite in habit and method, with whom he has worked in complete harmony these thirty-five years.

He finds a kindred soul in one Mr. Henri Gagnon, a picturesque gentleman of Gallic gallantry, who lives in Quebec and administers the affairs of a newspaper called *Le Soleil.*

He was once so affected by Mr. Gagnon's generosity of spirit that he endeavoured to express his superlative appreciation by offering, with richly embroidered emphasis, to associate himself with Mr. Gagnon's religious faith.

In spite of this intention, he has never actually been in a church of any description although he subscribes to one regularly in Winnipeg.

His subscription is attributed to the fact that the church has a weather vane which is visible from his bedroom window and which thus assists him each morning in determining the selection of his apparel for the day.

When he is obliged to visit Toronto he stops at the Ontario Club where the night staff immediately prepares for very little sleep.

Although he is only seventy-three or so, he is beginning to notice that he sometimes feels a little tired about four in the morning and is consequently convinced that the prairie climate wears men out quickly.

He thinks he does not work as hard as he used to and now rarely has more than five or six people lined up at his office door.

It embarrasses him to have attention drawn to the part he has played in making the *Free Press* a great newspaper or to his work in establishing The Canadian Press service of leased wires on which almost every daily paper in the country now relies.

His favourite flavour is essence of juniper. To this he likes to add a little lemon and soda but will take it plain rather than not at all.

He has an intimate and astounding knowledge of Canadian and British history which he endeavours to conceal except when it is needed.

On a wager with Sir Clifford Sifton he once endured a state of complete aridity for a period of some years and has often wondered how much harm this did him.

He has played safe ever since.

He has very definite views about anything one cares to mention and likes to tell people the opposite to what he believes to see whether they will be weak-minded enough to agree.

If he cannot start a satisfactory argument this way he will summon a subordinate, place in this victim's mouth a wholly indefensible statement and then assault it with suitable indignation.

He likes almost anything that is not good for him.

When invited to any function he reserves the right to enquire who will be there and, upon being informed, is apt to employ great emphasis in declining to attend.

As a host his conduct is a matter of artistry, no matter how unimportant his guest may be, and he never forgets a friend's birthday or the remotest form of anniversary.

He never loses his temper except when something annoys him.

When he does happen to become a little annoyed nobody ever hears anything about it except the people within three city blocks.

His major explosions occur when he encounters a news article in which he sees prejudice or untruth.

As an employer he is generous to the point of benevolence and practically nobody has been fired from the *Free Press* in the last thirty-five years.

He regards sixty to eighty miles an hour as normal motoring speed and does not understand why his chauffeurs usually quit within a few months.

His affection for the United States is such that he never crosses the border if he can possibly avoid it.

In politicians, his preference is for dead ones.

MISS MACPHAIL

June, 1933.

MISS AGNES MACPHAIL was born in a log cabin but has not yet become Prime Minister.

She spent the first fourteen years of her life on a farm in Grey County, Ontario, and looks back upon that period as being almost as bad as her last twelve years in Ottawa.

Her opinion of parliament is that a great deal of trouble and expense could be eliminated by letting most of the members stay at home and merely supply rubber stamps of their signatures.

She is a Latter Day Saint, a C.C.F., an inflationist, a free-trader, a central-banker, an anti-militarist and has often said so.

She would probably be a Liberal if she found the Liberal party less conservative.

She found it necessary to define her Latter Day Saintship when she first went to Ottawa because it had been rumoured that she believed in polygamy, although it is now well established that she is skeptical of matrimony in even its simplest form.

She believes that men who praise their wives need watching and she doubts if they are worth it.

She disposes of past romances by declaring that no woman with any pep reaches the age of thirty without having had proposals of marriage.

She is forty-odd years old now and doesn't care who knows it.

When she was nineteen she secured a position as school-teacher at Kinloss, Ontario and has admitted that she used to dance all night whenever she got a chance, although she does not enlarge on this to Mr. Woodsworth.

After this she became ill for a year and moved out to a school in Alberta where she acquired a supply of fresh air and new ideas.

She brought these back east to another school at Sharon.

a community not far from Toronto and chiefly inhabited at that time by political economists known as United Farmers of Ontario.

She completely recovered her health in this atmosphere, attracted attention by being rude to the Drayton Tariff Commission in 1920 and got her start in politics by writing a letter to the editor of the *Farmer's Sun* who has never completely recovered from the shock.

She won her first election in 1921 by a personal expenditure of two hundred dollars and a series of sharp remarks.

The election later proved to be expensive, however, as she felt obliged to return six thousand dollars of her parliamentary indemnity during the next four years in order to keep a campaign promise.

She prides herself on always saying what she thinks but occasionally has overlooked the importance of thinking what she says.

She barely squeezed through with a majority of 243 in the last election but expects to have no trouble at all in the next one.

She describes the depression as a transition from one era to another but unfortunately has not yet disclosed how long the interval will last.

Among her major difficulties are keeping quiet, getting homesick, and having to listen to professional politicians.

She is suspicious of people who are nice to her and dangerous to people who aren't.

She says that C.C.F. means Come Comrades Forward, which indicates that she had better let somebody else give the party its campaign slogan.

She would rather make an epigram than be right and sometime has.

In her first few years of parliament she was described by one of the cultured Toronto members as an ignorant little school-teacher and by the eminent Mr. Hector Charlesworth as pert, shallow and misinformed.

(Mr. Charlesworth is a former littérateur whom Mr. Bennett mistook for somebody else and who has since wished that he were.)

Since those days she has been Canadian delegate to the League of Nations and a member of the League's Disarmament Commission, and is now in danger of becoming a person of national importance.

She once said that Toronto has an odd mentality, a statement remarkable only for its extreme restraint.

Two of her early ambitions were to serve her constituents and to learn French, the latter being an inspiration once cherished by Senator Meighen who now best understands the kind of French that Mr. Bennett speaks.

She has discovered that the House of Commons is one of the nicest clubs in the country and that much of the business of government is conducted in the Chateau Laurier.

If she had her way she would abolish the senate except perhaps the Honourable George P. Graham.

She once danced with Mr. Henry Ford at Dearborn, Michigan, and subsequently described him as being something like Mr. Vincent Massey, a comparison which fails to make clear which gentleman, if either, she intended to compliment.

She has never been afraid of anyone and sometimes would rather like to be.

She has not yet learned that a politician should never write a letter dealing with any subject beyond the weather but, of course, she is not a politician except at election time.

She believes that newspapers, except the *Farmer's Sun*. are in some sort of capitalistic conspiracy to start another war and she intends to stop it.

She has blue eyes, black hair, red cheeks and a sharp temper.

If one-half the members of the House of Commons had one-half her rectitude and moral courage the others would not matter so much.

MR. MASSEY

August, 1933.

MR. VINCENT MASSEY is always active in something and usually a little anxious about it.

He is only forty-six years old (1933) but already has been a university professor, a colonel, a patron of the arts, an industrial magnate, a cabinet minister, a Hart House actor and a diplomat.

Of these, he and Mrs. Massey found that the most satisfactory was being a diplomat, even in Washington.

He is now engaged in politics as president of the National Federation of Liberal Associations, a position which includes the privilege of contributing whatever effort may be necessary to win the next election.

In this capacity he is regarded by imaginative persons as a sinister figure who plans presently to depose Mr. Mackenzie King, the Kingsmere nature-lover.

He is, however, quite content to let Mr. King be Prime Minister again and has absolutely no personal ambition in his present endeavours as long as he becomes the **next High Commissioner** in London.

He is five feet eight inches tall, weighs one hundred and thirty, has a Cuban complexion and is obliged to shave twice a day if he is doing anything in the evening, which he usually is.

He was born in Toronto, graduated from Varsity when he was twenty-three and then went over to Oxford to be educated. At Oxford he went in for rowing as a coxswain and made a detailed study of the river currents.

He came back from Oxford as a history professor at Varsity for a couple of years, grew a moustache and became a staff colonel when the war came along, went to Ottawa as secretary of the cabinet's War Committee and then was put in charge of repatriation.

He thinks bridge is a waste of time.

His first name is Charles but he never uses it because he fears that some people would call him Charlie.

After the war he decided to go into business so he joined the Massey-Harris Company, worked hard and was promoted to the presidency in 1921.

He stayed on as Massey-Harris president for four years and became so earnest about it that he wrote Mr. Arthur Meighen a private letter containing dangerous remarks about tariff policy.

When Mr. King made him a cabinet minister a few months later the letter was a little worrisome but it was not published (thanks to Sir Robert Borden) and he forestalled trouble by telling Mr. King all about it anyway.

He refers to Mr. King as Rex, a brevity which seems inadequate to other members of the party.

He is a cousin but hardly a friend of Mr. Denton Massey, the Toronto mesmerist, who lately has interested himself in advertising and believes that this activity, like charity, begins at home.

If he could borrow some of the bodily bulk which Mr. Denton Massey could readily spare and if he could lose some of his constant culture he might end up as Prime Minister whether he wanted to or not.

He would, at any rate, be better able to cope with Mr. Mitchell Hepburn, the Prairie Flower of Elgin County, whom he hopes to see installed as Premier of Ontario as one means to the greater end.

He would also have less inconvenience with Mr. Arthur Slaght, the Liberal impressario whose method of evening conference he has occasionally found a little disconcerting.

He resigned as president of Massey-Harris to avoid trouble in the 1925 election and insisted on running in Durham, Ontario, where his forefathers had started the agricultural implement business and where he owns a place called Batterwood, near Port Hope.

He delivered some excellent speeches on economics,

mixed with the people and lost the election by 650 votes and about sixteen thousand dollars.

He has one of the finest intellectual equipments in the country but is now beginning to realize that this is of little advantage in political matters.

He prides himself on being modest.

After the 1925 election he was uncertain about things for a year or so until Mr. King sent him to Washington as the first Canadian minister, a job for which he received twelve thousand a year and was obliged to spend fifty.

He is subject to sudden seizures of obstinacy but is perfectly reasonable about anything as long as he gets his own way.

Nobody could have done the Washington job better than he did and he really liked it down there, especially the summer months which he spent at Batterwood.

Before he went to Washington he sold out his Massey-Harris interest to Mr. J. H. Gundy. He accepted about eighty dollars a share and was quite willing to let Mr. Gundy feel pleased about it at that time.

He stuck it for four years at Washington, entertained the Willingdons there, survived other ordeals, and was gratified when he was duly rewarded in the spring of 1930 by being appointed to succeed the late Mr. Peter Larkin as High Commissioner in London.

He bought a London mansion in Park Lake and intended to sail in September, but this programme was slightly disarranged when Mr. Bennett won the election in July and decided to favour England with Mr. G. Howard Ferguson, a public servant who needed a change.

He has, however, kept the Park Lane house, hopes to be living in it within another year or so, and thinks how nice it might be some day to welcome the Duke of Calgary there.

In the meantime he is living at his place at Port Hope. He has a cabin in the garden where he does his correspondence and talks with people about the election.

SENATOR MEIGHEN

February, 1933.

SENATOR MEIGHEN occasionally reflects that things might be worse, but not very much.

One of the few things he likes about being Leader of the Senate is that he has no Board of Strategy to make suggestions about maintaining the dignity of a Prime Minister.

He considers it not wholly surprising that Mr. Bennett has no colleagues who can tell him anything.

He is still the most dexterous verbal swordsman in the country but finds little satisfaction in stabbing holes in stuffed shirts.

He is a historical demonstration that intellect in politics is a handicap rather than an advantage, unless accompanied by a sense of humour, a talent for dramatics, a capacity for bulldozing or all three.

He went to school in St. Mary's, Ontario, and there are times when he wishes he had stayed there.

After that he went through Toronto University and became a school teacher, a lawyer, a politician, a statesman, and a financier. He is not quite sure what he is now, but wishes he were something else.

Upon retrospective analysis, he considers that financiers are probably a little superior to politicians and that school teachers are better than either.

He is now not quite as sure as he was in 1928 that he is a great financier except by comparison.

After he gave up politics for finance he gained about twenty-five pounds and does not appear to be in serious danger of losing these in the duties attached to his present office.

He felt humiliated when people congratulated him upon his elevation to the Senate and even worse when they consoled him.

He believes that something should be done about the depression and favours re-establishing silver as a monetary

111

standard but as yet has not quite convinced Mr. Bennett, an Ottawa economist who is also interested in political affairs.

There are a number of things on which he has not yet convinced Mr. Bennett, and still more on which he has not even tried.

In all the years he has been in public life he believes that there has never been an instance when his memory has failed him as to fact or figure, but he is quite capable of appearing at a wedding in brown shoes and a top hat, if he remembers that there is a wedding and where it is being held.

He has lost some of the delightful uncertainty of his attire, but has not yet learned to put on his collar and tie properly or to wear a hat that does not look like an undertaker's.

He and Mr. Mackenzie King are the same age, and he is happy to believe that this is almost the only point of resemblance between them.

So is Mr. King.

Among other people whom he is glad he does not resemble too closely are Mr. Arthur Slaght, Miss Agnes Macphail, ex-Senator McDougald, Lady Willingdon and Sir Herbert Holt.

All his life he has been handicapped by the stupidity of his fellows and his inability to do anything about it.

He has never been able to resist making a sharp remark even when the circumstances required a dull one.

He is reputed to be one of the few men whose purposes Lloyd George was never able to divine but he has balanced this by being almost the only person who seems unable to make an accurate measurement of Senator Webster.

He is quite fond of dancing which he executes as a form of exercise.

He was officially a member of the Canadian delegation to the Imperial Economic Conference in Ottawa last year but was not called upon by Mr. Bennett to attend any of the sessions and is, in fact, only now finding out what really happened.

He admires rhetorical intricacies and on occasion has shown himself to be peculiarly susceptible to flattery concealed in verbiage.

He has inadequate judgment of character, and probably will never understand why Sir Arthur Currie would not accept the terms of his proposal to become a Member of his Cabinet.

His quality of mercy is a little strained.

He cherishes a strictly private and forlorn hope that, somehow and some day, there will a proper understanding and vindication of the "ready, aye ready" speech he once made in Hamilton, Ontario.

He can make a speech in French if he rehearses carefully but he has never had the Hamilton oration translated for that purpose.

He has pride without conceit and wit but no humour.

A great many people continue to regard him as the only great Canadian statesman since the war but they have probably overlooked the success of Mr. G. Howard Ferguson in saving England from degeneration.

The same people still hope that he will some day return to the House of Commons but it may be taken as quite definite that he will never do so unless a favourable opportunity occurs.

He is not quite sure what he would do if he were Prime Minister again, except that he would not have another Winnipeg convention.

COLONEL MOLSON

March, 1934.

COLONEL HERBERT MOLSON runs a brewery in Montreal, has almost as much money as Sir Herbert Holt, and is undoubtedly the most completely respectable citizen east of Toronto.

He is also head of Montreal General Hospital, a governor of McGill, a director of Bell Telephone and the Bank of Montreal, and a member of every notable club in the city except the Press Club.

He has never in his life done anything improper and probably never will but tries hard to be happy anyway.

He belongs to a fourth generation of a Lincolnshire family which settled in Montreal in 1782 and which ever since has personified propriety to such a distressing degree that, if its skeletons venture to rattle at all, they always give somebody else's name.

The first Montreal Molson is now officially referred to as John the Elder and his son is known as John the Younger. Between them they started the brewery, put the first steamship on the St. Lawrence, built the first railway in North America, founded one of the first banks and established a large fortune.

To both the brewery and the fortune the family has given such prudent attention for the last 150 years that each of these items has now a civic virtue equalled only by the Charity Ball.

The Colonel is descended from John the Elder's son Thomas, who had three sons. Two of these three sons were christened John as a precautionary measure in view of John the Elder's will which bequeathed the brewery to the grandson John who first attained majority.

Each of the brothers named John had his turn as head of the brewery and, the later of these being the Colonel's father, his own succession to the crown followed in due course in 1910.

He went to France in 1915, when he was forty years old, in command of a company in the 42nd Battalion, and did not return until 1919.

His activities during this period resulted in one wound, one Military Cross, one C.M.G., one mention in despatches and several staff appointments in which he rendered himself unique by displaying both diligence and intelligence.

He went through Montreal High School, graduated from McGill as a bachelor of arts and science in 1894 when he was nineteen, and a year later entered the brewery for post-graduate work, at which he has since made considerable progress.

He played football for McGill and still attends all the games at Molson Stadium which shows what punishment a really loyal McGill alumus is willing to take.

Any worthy charity can count on him for a substantial donation of his own money but he will spend hours investigating the smallest details of expenditures in order to cut the General Hospital's costs by two dollars a week.

His sense of humour is practically invisible except to himself.

He is over six feet tall, has blue eyes, blond hair and a little trouble with his weight which he periodically undertakes to correct by dieting until he loses ten pounds.

He then proceeds to regain these at once.

He likes apple pie and chicken à la king, eats them about four times a week and secretly would like to have them for breakfast.

He has lunch at the Mount Royal Club nearly every day but now and then drops into the St. James's Club when he is in a hurry and does not feel very particular.

He also plays bridge at the Mount Royal almost every afternoon and is ranked as a highly proficient exponent of the Vanderbilt system. This ranking, however, is only by Mount Royal Club standards.

He is also quite proficient at racquets but plays golf only when compelled by his friends, the more optimistic of whom calculate that by assiduous effort and enough good luck he may sometimes get around Mount Bruno in less than 120.

Apart from making money, his most skilful activity is salmon fishing for which purpose he has the Bonaventure Club on Chaleurs Bay.

He will listen to music if he has to, recognizes Wagner as one of the greatest shortstops in the history of the game, and regards the Molsoneers as infinitely superior to the New York Philharmonic.

At the brewery he works in an old office coat or sometimes in his shirt sleeves, this being the closest approach any member of the family has made to support the old adage about the three generations.

He has a large house on Ontario Avenue in Montreal, another in the Laurentians at Ivry, another on the St. Lawrence at Metis, and a yacht named the Curlew, all of which he uses for the edification of his friends.

He would rather entertain than be entertained and likes to take a party of men for a cruise down the river or for a winter weekend at Ivry, the chief activity on such occasions being mild sessions of bridge at a quarter of a cent.

In his more reckless moods he will sometimes go to a movie or read a detective story neither of which he always understands.

He smokes a pipe all day and has never been known to lose his temper even in dealing with the Government of Quebec.

He speaks French with a Bank of Montreal accent.

He studies everything he undertakes to the smallest detail and in France once won a bet from one of his subalterns by being able to call by name every man in the latter's platoon.

It is never safe to tell him anything at random because he will not forget about it and is quite apt to challenge one with it three years later.

He practises moderation to excess.

SIR WILLIAM

August, 1933.

SIR WILLIAM MULOCK is a very venerable old man who lives in Toronto and is the only citizen of that city whom all four of its newspapers treat with respect.

He has a bigger and better white beard than Sir Joseph Flavelle and is almost as wise as this makes him appear.

He dislikes publicity so intensely that he will never consent to be interviewed by a reporter more than once a day.

He was born in Ontario at a place called Bondhead, went to Grammar School nearby in Newmarket and graduated from Toronto University three years before confederation.

Then he spent a year at the Royal Military School in Toronto, took law at Osgoode Hall and was called to the bar in 1868.

He went into politics fourteen years later, when he was thirty-eight, and was Liberal member from North York for the next twenty-three years.

He wears old-fashioned spectacles and takes them off when he wants to read.

Sir Wilfrid Laurier took him into the Cabinet of All the Talents in 1896 as Postmaster-General in which capacity he introduced penny postage within the Empire and was knighted for doing it.

Later he became the first Canadian Minister of Labour and started his young friend, Mr. Mackenzie King, in public life by appointing him his first Deputy Minister.

He became one of Sir Wilfrid's closest friends and used to have an inflexible programme of three games of piquet with Lady Laurier every day after lunch.

He likes porridge for breakfast and has it every second morning.

He is also fond of sausages, gladioli, bridge and compliments.

He retired from politics and became an Ontario judge

in 1905, when he was sixty-one. He felt that he ought to do this because he was getting pretty old and his health was not very good.

He is now eighty-nine (1933) and his health is so bad that he smokes cigars right after breakfast, goes fishing in the rain and is apt to go out for the evening at midnight if somebody does not stop him.

He thinks Mr. Bennett is a promising young man.

After he retired in 1905 he carried on as a judge for eighteen years and then was made Chief Justice of Ontario. The next year he was also made Chancellor of Toronto University.

He has held these positions for only nine or ten years and is hardly accustomed to them yet.

His persistent virility, demonstrated over a considerable period, has brought envy to his juniors.

He is still seen at more public functions than any other figure in Toronto history with the possible exception of Mr. Thomas L. Church who is now chiefly remarkable because he is hardly seen at all.

He had acute appendicitis when he was seventy-nine and dislocated his shoulder in a fall the next year, but does not expect anything further to happen to him for some time to come.

He is disrespectfully suspected of chewing tobacco.

When he was Postmaster-General he met a young Italian inventor, named Marconi, and was persuaded to build a station at Glace Bay, Nova Scotia, where the world's first trans-Atlantic wireless message was received.

He thinks that worry is mankind's greatest ailment and is very worried about it.

He lives in a large house on Jarvis Street and has a highly dignified library filled with extremely uncomfortable chairs. He sits there each evening to read "Bringing Up Father".

He also has a three hundred acre farm near Aurora and is known in this locality as The Squire of Mulock's Corners.

He flies a flag to signify his presence at the farm where he has been noted for raising Shetland ponies, black walnut trees and other things.

He has ventured into several large real estate transactions in Toronto but is quite indifferent about the money he thus manages to make as long as he makes enough.

He may always be observed at the Woodbine Jockey Club on King's Plate Day attired in a rather odd top hat, white waistcoat, gold-headed stick and a long cigar.

In religion he is an Anglican and is thus one of the few Toronto citizens to achieve civic eminence without benefit of Methodism.

He tried nearly forty years ago to do away with railway passes for Members of Parliament and has always insisted on paying his own fare, a method of expressing political conviction which has not yet occurred to Mr. Woodsworth.

He also tried in parliament to obtain a fifty per cent. reduction of the Governor-General's salary but now is obliged to substitute for the Lieutenant-Governor of Ontario whenever that office is vacant, which quite a number of people think is not often enough.

He regards Toronto's Communists as a very serious menace and will not quite admit that the Chief of Police may be a worse one.

He has acquired a good deal of the formulaic outlook and opinion with which a Leading Citizen of Toronto must be equipped but manages to retain a saving proportion of his liberal instincts.

As a judge he once raised the question of whether an automobile is a necessity or a luxury and suggested that the country would be better off if all automobiles were laid up for a year.

The people of Oshawa immediately did not send him a vote of thanks.

He intends to write his memoirs when he becomes old enough.

MR. RHODES

November, 1933.

MR. EDGAR NELSON RHODES is Mr. Bennett's Minister of Finance but would rather go fishing.

He is tall, suave, facile and informed and remains habitually unruffled even when blamed for governmental conduct which he himself dislikes.

He was born in Amherst, Nova Scotia and still feels that this was wise.

He is undoubtedly one of the most deficient politicians Nova Scotia has ever produced for he has no talent whatever in slapping backs and, in the presence of infants, entirely lacks that osculatory enthusiasm without which no man can hope to attain high public office.

He has, nevertheless, won every election he has contested, ranks now as the Conservative heir apparent and, if he is not more careful, may some day become Prime Minister.

He is rated by some experts as one of the ten most effective orators in Canada, the other nine being presumably the man who persuaded the city of Montreal to install traffic lights.

He took arts at Acadia University and law at Dalhousie but preferred football at both.

In common with every young male bearing his family name he was known at school as Dusty although he was also rated as the sartorial superlative of the day wherever he appeared.

He has retained this reputation by being since regarded as the best dressed member in House of Commons' history which is probably not quite fair to Mr. Bennett's tailor.

After he finished Dalhousie he practised law for ten years, discovered that this was long enough for anybody and decided to try something easier.

He thereupon had himself elected to parliament in 1908, when he was thirty-one years old and found among his fellow freshmen at Ottawa two aspirants of similar youth named Meighen and King.

His Liberal opponent in 1908 was a great friend of his named Ralston. They grew up together in Amherst, have pretended to fight each other ever since, and now face each other in parliament as Finance Minister versus Finance Critic.

He has today a higher regard for Mr. Ralston than for some of his cabinet colleagues which perhaps is not so difficult to understand.

When the war started he conducted a recruiting campaign with his friend Ralston in Nova Scotia and was preparing to go overseas in 1916 when Sir Robert Borden interfered by making him Deputy Speaker of the House.

He was promoted to Speaker in 1917, proved to be the only man ever able to squelch Sir Sam Hughes, and consequently was kept in the Chair for the next four years.

Among the members of the House of Commons Press Gallery, he is still reputed to be the best Speaker parliament has had.

(The Press Gallery consists of a number of close-mouthed gentlemen who realize that they could run the country better than any elected government.)

He is one of the best bridge players in the country and was once invited to play by radio with Mr. Work but has thus far restrained himself from writing a book or even inventing a score pad.

After thirteen years of politics he finally, definitely and irrevocably retired in 1921 and took the presidency of a since deceased concern called the British American Nickel Corporation.

In the twelve years since he retired he has kept strictly out of politics except for five years as Premier of Nova Scotia, a couple of years as Mr. Bennett's Minister of Fisheries and a year or so as Minister of Finance.

When he really does come out of retirement he should be quite a help to The Party.

He became Premier of Nova Scotia in 1925, being so impelled to save the province that he displaced the Conservative leader of the day, and then proceeded to turn out a Liberal government which had lasted for forty-three years.

He won every seat in the legislature except three, but when he staged another election in 1928 he lost almost all this majority, which indicates what fun it is to be a politician in Nova Scotia.

He belongs to the Baptist Church, has two children and keeps these circumstances pretty well in mind except during the salmon season.

In 1927 he was one of several eminent gentlemen who were press-agented as successor to Mr. Arthur Meighen and was, in fact, more prominently mentioned than the present repository of the nation's hopes.

He made no effort to obstruct Mr. Bennett's sacrifice to public duty but was persuaded to become Minister of Fisheries after the great victory in 1930.

The only thing he liked about being Minister of Fisheries was the pleasant recollection which the name aroused. What he now likes about being Minister of Finance he has not discovered.

He dislikes people who fish with worms, rabid Grits, rabid Tories, parsnips, baggy trousers, cabinet meetings, income tax collectors, work, uncontrollable expenditures and being described as a golfer.

Next to salmon fishing he likes friends, books, hills, woods, good clothes, generosity, walking, meditation, tolerance and having nothing much to do.

In parliament he occupies the somewhat dangerous position of being as well liked by the Liberal members as by the Conservatives, partly because he answers the furthest back bencher with the same unfailing courtesy which he accords the most dangerous of his contemporaries.

He still thinks of Ottawa as being in Upper Canada, though only in a geographical sense.

MR. RICHARDSON

January, 1934.

MR. JAMES ARMSTRONG RICHARDSON lives in Winnipeg, is head of a grain company called James Richardson & Sons, and was publicly regarded as the Midas of the West until he went off the gold standard.

In the ten years between 1919 and 1929 he accumulated probably more money than any other man in Canada has made during a similar period and then proceeded to demonstrate that he could travel in reverse with equal celerity.

He was forty-four years old in 1929, was reported to have made ten millions in Nickel alone, and had a fortune estimated as at least level with Sir Herbert Holt's.

A surprising feature of his accumulation is that few critics have ever accused him of achieving it unfairly and, what is even more unique among financiers, there appear to be quite a number of people who will feel pleased when he fully regains it.

The explanation of these phenomena is probably the fact that, in the proper St. James Street sense, he is not a financier at all as he has been known on several occasions to treat distressed investors with consideration.

He is the fourth of his family to be president of the Richardson company, having been preceded by his grandfather, his father and his uncle.

His grandfather started the company ten years before confederation in Kingston, Ontario, a community notable for its two co-educational institutions, both of which have several talented graduates.

A third institution of the city is a cultural establishment known as the Royal Military College to which Miss Agnes Macphail undoubtedly intends to bequeath her entire estate.

His grandfather began by doing a nice business exporting Ontario barley to the United States but this disappeared

127

when Washington put through the Dingley tariff in 1894.

His father then decided to see what might be done in the western grain trade and his uncle followed by making the company the chief instrument of the greatest wheat exporting area in the world.

He was brought up in the company himself, did not escape from Kingston until he was twenty-two and then moved to the Toronto office, a change of doubtful improvement.

He stayed in Toronto, however, for only five years, went out to the company's headquarters in Winnipeg as vice-president in 1912 and now hardly ever comes east except when he wants some money.

For war service, he was commandeered by the government in 1918 to superintend distribution of wheat to some three hundred flour mills in Eastern Canada and probably should have been made a brigadier-general or a colonel at least.

He became president and general manager of the Richardson company in 1919 when he was thirty-four and was soon recognized as the biggest man in the west which meant that he had the most money.

He thereupon was made a director of the C.P.R., Hudson's Bay Company, International Nickel and other worthy enterprises but does not really enjoy the meetings very much, his chief contribution to such assemblies being an exhortation that they quit talking and do something.

He is also a director of the Canadian Bank of Commerce and gets along pretty well with Sir Joseph as neither of them smokes or drinks and both of them know how to make money.

He used to have to do his buying secretly because so many people followed him in the market but has not been troubled about this so much recently.

He enjoyed doing things that made money, will probably do them again sometime and in the meanwhile is as undisturbed about his losses as he was unexcited about his winnings.

He is still so busy with various large interests that he hardly ever gets time for any sport except hunting, golf, tennis, fishing, riding, sailing and anything else that lets him get outside.

He is six feet high, rugged, simple, genuine and so nearly good looking that he has been almost forced to notice it himself.

He lives amid some of Winnipeg's most distinguished citizens on Wellington Crescent and has a nice little house containing a swimming pool.

He also has a farm out on St. Mary's Road and likes to get out there in the summer time to potter around the barn when he is supposed to be busy at the office.

Another of his properties consists of a large hole in the ground surrounded by a high board fence at Portage and Main where the erection of the new office building has been a little delayed.

He still has his big office on the tenth floor of the Winnipeg Grain Exchange and likes to look out of the windows over the Red River and the stretch of prairie beyond.

He got into aviation during the boom as the quickest way to open up Northern Manitoba mining fields, has been president of Canadian Airways Limited since 1930, and takes more pride in his pilots than in anything else.

He is Chancellor of Queen's University but does not pretend to be much of an academician and is the sort of man whose friends are apt to refrain from giving him a book at Christmas because he already has one.

He is not much interested in politics either, but has visited Ottawa to explain grain matters to various parliamentary committees which, after their usual custom, have done the opposite to what he has advised.

He believes the West is God's country, likes to act as he thinks a Westerner should and tries accordingly to make the handclasp a little stronger.

MR. SISE

May, 1934.

MR. CHARLES FLEETFORD SISE is president of the Bell Telephone Company and lives in Montreal except when he goes away for a holiday.

He gives the company his earnest attention throughout the customary hours of the day and has thus achieved what is probably the most efficiently conducted enterprise in the country.

He would be quite content if nobody ever heard of him and, in this respect, appears to have succeeded so well as to distress some of his associates.

His name is pronounced to rhyme with Rice.

He became a director of the Bank of Montreal last year but has not yet been heard to admit his gratification.

He so greatly dislikes to see his name in print that he would not allow it to appear on the corner stone of the new telephone building in Montreal, an example of diffidence which is thoroughly offset by the presidential inscription upon the base of a large insurance building a couple of blocks away.

He is solid, stolid, sound and safe.

He is also notably addicted to good music to which he devotes both time and, when necessary, money.

He does not expect the elevator girls in his building to recognize him and almost hopes they won't, in which respect he differs from some other directors of his company.

His ancestors came from Cork and were men of the sea. The first Sise to cross the Atlantic reached shore in a rowboat after twice being shipwrecked and thereupon entered the shipbuilding business.

His father, at twenty, was captain of the clipper ship "Annie Sise", carried supplies to the Crimea for Great Britain, ran the blockade for the Southern States during the Civil War and was forty-five before settling in Montreal to start the telephone company.

His pride in his father is one of the sentiments which

131

his caution conceals, but he keeps a picture of the "Annie Sise" upon the wall facing his desk and looks at it when there is nobody around.

He does not like draughts, cold soup, jazz, back-slapping, subtlety, Christmas cigars or anything else which interferes with organized comfort.

He is highly cautious in all his conduct and, upon being invited to a party, his inclination is to enquire who else will be there before committing himself.

He will not make a speech of any kind if he can avoid it and still wonders how he was one year persuaded to act as president of the Canadian Club.

He lives part way up Mount Royal in a thirteen-roomed apartment at 1400 McGregor Street, an excessively respectable structure familiarly known as the Grain Elevator.

He leads a life typical of Montreal but not well understood in certain other communities where the belief prevails that leisure contradicts accomplishment.

He keeps two or three automobiles and likes to drive them himself, this being probably his closest approach to adventure except when he goes fishing.

He permits himself to go fishing only when he feels like it and strictly limits himself to trout at Mattewan and salmon on the Pabos unless he hears of a new place to try.

He considers that golf is all right and plays it with due decorum at Dixie and Mount Bruno.

His generous inclinations are handicapped by his fear that someone will get a chance to thank him.

Among his friends he is never neglectful of his own interest and has a talent for making himself comfortable under any circumstances.

He went to Lincoln College at Sorel and Bishop's College School at Lennoxville, graduated from McGill as an electrical engineer when he was twenty-two and has been in the telephone business ever since.

He became assistant general manager of the telephone company when he was twenty-nine, general superintendent at thirty-two, general manager at thirty-seven and president in 1925 when he was fifty.

He has now reached the age of almost sixty, but has done this so unobtrusively that few of his friends have noticed.

He reaches his office each morning about nine-thirty and thereupon engages in reading *The Gazette,* a morning opiate supplied by a local philanthropist.

At ten minutes to one he walks around the corner to the St. James's Club for lunch, where he wonders how far he can go without violating the dietary mandates to which he is occasionally adjured.

The St. James's'is a somewhat airless institution having two classes of members: those who wish they belonged to the Mount Royal Club and those who are glad they don't belong to the Mount Stephen.

At five o'clock he proceeds to the Mount Royal Club for bridge, a form of endeavour which many of the members regard as the really serious business of the day.

In his bridge he likes to employ an abstruse method of valuation which he calls the Biltmore Count but to which his partners frequently apply a different descriptive.

He occasionally varies his afternoon schedule by going to the Montreal Tennis Club where he finds satisfaction in his forehand drive, this being a subject of comment among the members whenever it works.

He is quite apt to pass an acquaintance on the street without salute rather than run the risk of saying something silly, a form of shyness which has caused a number of observers to refer to him in erroneous terms of reproach.

He has an unbending sense of justice and a mind so literal in its honesty that he cannot fool even himself.

His instinctive course through life is the line of least resistance but he makes decisions with a finality which leaves no room for uncertainty.

It is highly improbable that he will ever suffer a nervous breakdown.

MR. STEVENS

November, 1934.

MR. HENRY HERBERT STEVENS is a political Saint George who thought his latest dragon was behaving in a satisfactory manner until it suddenly turned around and bit him.

He is accustomed to engage in such encounters well mounted upon a cabinet horse and is beginning to find it somewhat awkward to continue the combat on foot.

As yet, however, he has found no satisfactory way to remount and is consequently obliged to depend on a halo which may lose its lumination a little too soon.

His resignation from the Cabinet makes his political future so clear that there is still quite a chance of his eventually becoming Conservative leader unless he is meanwhile ejected from the party altogether.

In his recent activities to save the common people some observers have discerned personal strategy, but it would probably be more fair to say that any element of stage play soon became a reality in which his zeal now reaches obsession.

He views life as a serious business, plays no games, has no pastimes, and hardly ever wastes a moment except at economics.

He has nearly always found something wrong and is a little unhappy when he does not.

He enjoys argument to such an extent that he has succeeded in convincing himelf of some surprising conclusions.

He is fifty-six years old, has been in politics since he was thirty-three and may be counted upon to retire about the same time that Mr. Mackenzie King carries out his policy of senate reform.

If he ever does retire from politics there are a number of jobs he might get but these possibilities do not seem to include an appointment as public relations counsel to The T. Eaton Co.

This job will be open to him about the same day that

135

Mr. Bennett offers to send him to London as High Commissioner.

He was born in Bristol, England, came out to Canada when he was nine and settled in Peterborough, an Ontario community not far from Lindsay.

He liked Peterborough so well that as soon as he had finished public school there he moved to British Columbia, tried his luck at gold mining, drove a mountain stage coach and graduated as a railway fireman.

When this became too easy he thought he would try the army, so he went to the United States and enlisted in the infantry for service in China during the Boxer rebellion.

After he had been marched to Peking he was shipped south to help conquer the Phillipines, took a cruise on his own through the South Sea Islands and found adventure so monotonous that he was obliged to return to Vancouver.

By way of change he decided to experiment in business, got a job in an accountant's office, studied on the side and in due time became an accountant himself.

At the same time, he acquired views of so radical a nature that he felt sure he was a Socialist and resolved that he must devote himself to Public Service whenever an opportunity occurred.

In order to give opportunity a decent chance he shed the Socialist label and became known as a Conservative, a transmutation which he found quite logical as he has believed both creeds to be based upon faith in the omnipotence of government.

He became a leading member of the Good Government League in Vancouver, got into his first fight in a bitter crusade against the city's liquor interests and found himself elected to the city council when he was thirty-two.

The Dominion election on Reciprocity came along the next year and as the Vancouver Conservatives saw no chance of victory they invited him to be the candidate.

He could not decline this further opportunity to benefit mankind, so accepted, won the seat by the largest majority

Vancouver had recorded up to that time, and has been in the House of Commons ever since.

He won Vancouver in each election from 1911 to 1930 when he was defeated by Mr. Ian Mackenzie, a Celtic gentleman who knows how to stimulate an audience.

He was, however, quickly restored to public life when Mr. Bennett journeyed to Vancouver and found him his present seat in Kootenay East, this being an example of solicitude which may now be expected to operate in reverse with equal despatch.

During the last twenty years he has engaged in admittedly highminded endeavours against Asiatic immigration, the high cost of living, combines and profits, the United Grain Growers and evil odours in the Customs department, with a noticeable improvement in his vocabulary and parliamentary manner.

He started his latest crusade last January (1934) against Mass Buyers, Price Spreads and Prominent People and it is now likely that it will prove a great success if Parliament is not dissolved before the report is ready.

His fervor for state regulation of business has horrified his Cabinet contemporaries but they may be obliged to borrow it as their chief hope before the next election.

He has a dimple in his chin, does not smoke, drink, swear or gamble and is moderate in all his habits except oratory and correspondence, two activities in which he employs the same degree of discretion.

He is unique in a number of respects, one of these being the fact that he is virtually the only subject upon which the present Cabinet has been voluntarily unanimous.

He feels that virtue is its own reward but sometimes cannot avoid being a little envious of certain acquaintances who have managed to have it accompanied by more tangible results.

Of the last three Conservative Prime Ministers he prefers Sir Robert Borden and Mr. Arthur Meighen.

He wears wing collars but drives his own car.

137

MR. TASCHEREAU

February, 1934.

MR. LOUIS ALEXANDRE TASCHEREAU is frequently referred to as the last surviving aristocrat in Canadian public life, a description which seems to overlook both the Mayor of Montreal and the Chairman of the Radio Commission.

He is also known to newspapers as The Grand Seigneur of Quebec and takes a kindly interest in the welfare of simple old habitants like the Honourable Gordon Scott and Mr. George Montgomery.

He is undoubtedly the best premier Quebec has had for at least thirteen years.

His family came out to New France from Tours in 1727 and have been here ever since, which indicates that Canada is not quite as new as the *Vancouver Sun* sometimes seems to think.

One of his family fought under Montcalm, another was in the first parliament of Lower Canada, another was the first cardinal of Quebec and another was the father of thirty-six children.

He was born in Quebec, went through the Seminary and Laval University, was a lawyer at twenty-two and a city alderman soon after.

He made his first try at politics in 1892 when he was twenty-five years old, but was defeated. He waited eight years, tried again, and has never since lost an election.

He liked being a lawyer and is probably more proud of being regarded as a good attorney-general than of ranking as a successful premier.

He is now sixty-seven (1934) and to rumours of his retirement during the past few years has invariably replied that, as he gave up his law to serve in politics, he intends to stay where he is as long as he retains health and public confidence.

His last election campaign was in 1931 when he obtained the biggest majority on record, thus maintaining the

Quebec government as the oldest administration in the world today.

If he ever stops being premier of Quebec there are a number of jobs open to him but one of them is not likely to be with the American Newspaper Publishers' Association.

He is five feet ten inches tall, weighs one hundred and forty, is supposed by some to be quite frail and has the physical constitution of a Rocky Mountain goat.

He has endured a routine of work year after year which would flatten out some of our more robust statesmen within six months.

He works at his office five nights a week and, when he attends a dinner party, often leaves at ten o'clock in order to get back to his desk for a while.

One night five years ago when he went back to his office he narrowly escaped being blown up by a stick of dynamite, placed there by an individual who apparently realized that this is the only method by which he will ever be put out of office.

He spends each Tuesday at the Government offices in Montreal in order to keep urban electors feeling happy and was once rewarded by having twelve hundred dollars stolen from his clothes in the Place Viger hotel.

He has gradually recovered this loss by devoting his Tuesday evenings to the instruction of certain Montreal gentlemen in the art of poker and often wishes that his Quebec train departed at a later hour.

He follows a rule of never being away from his office for more than one week at a time since he finds that a good deal of trouble can accumulate during that interval.

He has kept away from doctors for the last fifty years.

He lives in Quebec on a street called Grand Allee but is never quite as far from Montreal's St. James Street as these geographical circumstances would indicate.

He walks home for lunch every day, calls at the Garrison Club for an appetizer before dinner and always has something to eat before he goes to bed, which shows the irregular habits some of these politicians have.

He talks English in jerks, a method which gives him time to think even though he doesn't need it.

He had an audience with the Pope in 1926 and has also seen Mr. Bennett several times.

He has not, however, emulated Mr. Bennett in sacrificing his private interests upon the altar of public duty and continues to act as director of numerous enterprises, including three life insurance companies, a bank, a trust company and The Seigniory Club.

He likes to go to fires and keeps a fire alarm guide in his desk to aid in the pursuit.

He has little use for golf and regards bridge as a time-killer for people who are too stupid to converse intelligently.

He is, however, an expert billards player and is still one of the best fly-fishermen in the province, having once taken twenty-eight salmon in a single day.

He also has a hunting lodge at St. Joachim where he has entertained various governors-general, presumably to refresh them from the fatigue occasioned by the arduous duties of their office.

Whenever things become a little dull he can turn to the newsprint industry with complete certainty of immediate diversion.

He has a supply of courage which mounts as a fight progresses.

He once called Miss Agnes Macphail a foolish young girl and she did her best to be annoyed.

He sternly condemns sectionalism and will have nothing to do with racial or religious discord except at election time.

For political purposes he maintains reasonably close contact with federal Liberals, but for some of them he has an esteem about as warm as that which he and Mr. Meighen used to enjoy.

He is charming to talk with, always remembers his friends, and never forgets an enemy.

MR. TOWERS

October, 1934.

MR. GRAHAM F. TOWERS is a tall, shrewd young man from Montreal who is never surprised by anything.

He was not surprised, to any visible degree, even when he found himself elected to be Governor of the new Central Bank, his composure perhaps being due to his acquaintance with the qualifications of other rumoured possibles.

He thinks he will like Ottawa quite well except for the poor train service to Montreal.

He never counts chickens before they are hatched and remains very skeptical about them afterwards.

He wears a highly varnished protection of complete imperturbability even during post-midnight periods in the Villa Maurice, a Montreal institution of refined entertainment occasionally patronized by young bankers.

He has a disconcerting practice of gazing at one with eyes which do not blink through rimless glasses which never need polishing.

At such moments of appraisal he displays all the warmth of human emotion which might be associated with an electric adding machine operating in a sub-zero temperature.

If he did not wear glasses and were less tall he would look a little like the Prince of Wales, although he has never ridden to hounds in his life.

He has a talent for agreeable conversation which has deluded many hopeful gentlemen into believing that they were making excellent progress until they reached the point of mentioning what they were after.

At this point he suddenly develops all the loquacity of an oyster with sleeping sickness.

He is never untidy, never hurried and never enthusiastic.

His nearest approach to outward enthusiasm has probably been upon returning from skiing to a comfortably warm room supplied with those amenities which a gentleman likes to expect when roughing it in the mountains.

143

He looks like a better bridge player than he really is.

His sense of humour takes the form of a delicate and appreciative irony which misses no opportunity for exercise.

He was born in Montreal, went to Montreal High School and thus had no contact with real culture until he was sent to Toronto to attend St. Andrew's College.

He so keenly appreciated the difference between the two cities that, immediately upon finishing St. Andrew's, he registered at McGill.

He did not finish McGill until 1919 due to a military interlude of three years, during which he fitted himself for banking by becoming intimately familiar with the habit and behaviour of the Army Service Corps mule.

He graduated from McGill in political economy, intended to become a lawyer and went to The Royal Bank in 1920 more or less by accident when a friend of his turned down the new-fangled job of economist and passed it along to him.

The Bank soon found him too good to be true and much too sensible to be a real economist, so he was shipped to Havana as an accountant in 1922, promoted to inspector of Cuban branches in 1923 and inspector of all foreign branches in 1924.

This job took him to London, Paris, Barcelona and other centres of interest but was not as entertaining as it sounded since it required him to spend dizzy night hours counting securities in musty vaults while his travelling companions occupied themselves in nearby places of amusement.

It was too late then for him to become a lawyer, so he stuck it out and in 1929 was moved back to Montreal as Chief Inspector of the Bank, a title whose exact meaning he was never able to ascertain.

The promotion was, however, quite satisfactory as it brought him into the rarified atmosphere of the inner group on the Second Floor at Head Office, a happy little family always ready to help anyone in trouble as long as the collateral is sound.

Two years later he was made assistant to the general manager, which left him still in some uncertainty as to his duties but with no doubt about his working hours.

Last year he became assistant general manager and the Bank was getting into the embarrassing position of having no more promotions to offer him when Mr. Bennett relieved the situation in September.

His appointment as Governor of the Bank of Canada is for seven years, this being a relief to his friends who have been getting fed-up with being obliged to congratulate him on promotions every few months.

He is now being described as an economist again but will probably manage to disprove this before it goes too far.

He has a clear, clipped manner of speaking which makes him interesting even when he talks about nothing, which a banker sometimes does.

He has for several years belonged to an intellectual organization in Montreal known as the Twenty Club, a group of supposedly bright young men who gather at dinner twice a month during the winter to seek improvement by self-inflicted oratory.

He smokes cigarettes and would look silly with a pipe.

He exhibits a sharp temper when it seems advantageous to do so but usually contradicts people with a meticulous courtesy which permits no quarrel.

Nobody who knows him has doubt as to the painless ease with which he will extract the incisors of any carnivorous gentlemen at Ottawa.

He remembers everything he hears and believes very little of it.

He was thirty-seven at the end of September (1934) and looks even younger though probably not for long now.

At school he was much better at languages than at mathematics but quickly learned that arithmetic does not matter much in banking as long as one is careful always to make his mistakes on the right side.

He likes Saturday nights.

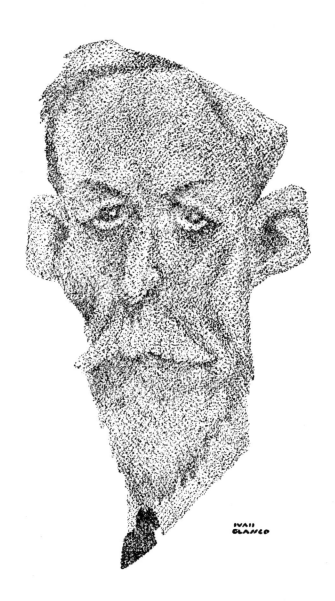

MR WOODSWORTH

February, 1933.

MR. JAMES SHAVER WOODSWORTH comes from Winnipeg, has a talent for becoming prominent whenever times are bad but is merely another Member of Parliament when times are good.

He has lately received so much public attention as to indicate that the country is in terrible shape and it is now understood that if things really collapse he will automatically become Prime Minister.

In this event, two probable members of the new cabinet would be Mr. Heaps, a faithful fellow-orator from Winnipeg who has remained undismayed throughout successive capitalistic regimes, and Mr. Henri Bourassa, the greatest nearly-was in Canadian politics.

Another probable Minister of the Crown would be Miss Agnes Macphail, a militant anti-militarist who is unquestionably the most distinguished woman member the House of Commons has ever had.

A number of people are convinced that he got into this country from Russia, receives monthly pay cheques from Moscow, and is concealing within the mouthful of the Co-operative Commonwealth Federation the deadly instrument of our destruction.

His family, however, was United Empire Loyalist and he took care to be born in Toronto, to attend Oxford and marry a Toronto University graduate, a combination of antecedent and attainment almost irreproachable enough to qualify him as President of the Empire Club.

He likes anything which he is told he can't have.

After he had finished with Oxford and subsequent items of education he started in, about thirty years ago, as a Methodist minister and still wears the beard with which he suited the part in his Winnipeg pulpit.

The beard has been advanced as conclusive evidence of his Soviet sympathies, but an explanation more commonly accepted by his acquaintances is that he retains it to camouflage his ears, which have occasionally attracted attention by their rather distinctive architecture.

Except for the beard he is not a particularly sinister figure, his general appearance being more or less that of a Passion Play performer.

He has, however, the loudest, strongest and most inescapable voice in the House of Commons as he will fully demonstrate before the present session of Parliament is over.

He proved rather dull as a preacher but stirred up considerable Methodist excitement by resigning from the church at regular intervals in protest against its doctrines.

One of the things he objected to was the Methodist belief in the general wickedness of the theatre, and he indicated his own opinion by shocking his parishioners with recommendations of certain theatrical performances which he thought might benefit them.

He resigned twice over this and other matters of denominational decree, but was re-instated both times and did not finally part company with Methodism until his third resignation in 1918, when he announced his opinion that the church should not encourage war.

He also wrote a letter to the editor of the Winnipeg *Free Press* protesting against conscription and promptly lost a nice Government position he had held.

He concluded that if he wanted to make a living it would perhaps be better to leave Winnipeg, so he trekked with his family to Vancouver and got a wheelbarrow job on the docks there.

In addition to being a minister and a dock hand, he has been a school teacher, an editor, a social service worker and a labour organizer and is now either a statesman or a public menace according to one's frame of mind.

It can hardly be said that he is a politician since no politician worthy of the name would handicap a new party with a descriptive label like Co-op-er-ative Com-mon-wealth Fed-er-ation.

Even a Board of Strategy probably knows better than that.

When he returned to Winnipeg from Vancouver times were getting bad and he at once became prominent by going to jail for writing what was said to be seditious libel during the Big Strike.

Part of the alleged sedition proved to be an excerpt from the Book of Isaiah. This was a little embarrassing to the authorities, so he was quickly released from jail and the charge was withdrawn.

Two years after this minor incident he was elected to Parliament as Labour Member for Centre Winnipeg, and he has been an affliction to each Government of the past eleven years.

He is undoubtedly a very awkward person to have in Parliament because he has practically no pastime except arguing about things, and has the additional fault of not being afraid of anybody or anything.

He is also the stubbornest Member of the House with one notable exception.

He is now quite certain that the C.C.F. would be completely successful if it were not for its supporters.

He had the faculty of irritating Mr. Meighen in debate with greater success than any other members of that day with the possible exceptions of Mr. Motherwell and Mr. Dunning both of whom, however, tried much harder.

He is still somewhat Methodistical in his style of oratory but has made one or two of the best speeches Parliament has heard in recent years.

He has also made one or two of the worst.

If he now has any preference in statesmen, he perhaps still rates Mr. King a bit ahead of Mr. Bennett, in the same sense that a man who is very fond of onions may like apples better than pears.